HOUSING FINANCE

THE CHANGING DOMESTIC PRIORITIES SERIES

Listed below are the titles published to date in the Changing Domestic Priorities Series

THE REAGAN EXPERIMENT
An Examination of Economic and Social Policies under the Reagan Administration (1982), John L. Palmer and Isabel V. Sawhill, editors

HOUSING ASSISTANCE FOR OLDER AMERICANS
The Reagan Prescription (1982), James P. Zais, Raymond J. Struyk, and Thomas Thibodeau

MEDICAID IN THE REAGAN ERA
Federal Policy and State Choices (1982), Randall R. Bovbjerg and John Holahan

WAGE INFLATION
Prospects for Deceleration (1983), Wayne Vroman

OLDER AMERICANS IN THE REAGAN ERA
Impacts of Federal Policy Changes (1983), James R. Storey

FEDERAL HOUSING POLICY AT PRESIDENT REAGAN'S MIDTERM
(1983), Raymond J. Struyk, Neil Mayer, John A. Tuccillo

STATE AND LOCAL FISCAL RELATIONS IN THE EARLY 1980s
(1983), Steven D. Gold

THE DEFICIT DILEMMA
Budget Policy in the Reagan Era (1983), Gregory B. Mills and John L. Palmer

HOUSING FINANCE
A Changing System in the Reagan Era (1983), John A. Tuccillo with John L. Goodman, Jr.

HOUSING FINANCE

A CHANGING SYSTEM IN THE REAGAN ERA

John A. Tuccillo

with John L. Goodman, Jr.

The Changing Domestic Priorities Series
John L. Palmer and Isabel V. Sawhill, Editors

THE URBAN INSTITUTE PRESS · WASHINGTON, D.C.

2100 M Street, N.W.
Washington, D.C. 20037

Library of Congress Cataloging in Publication Data

Tuccillo, John A.
Housing finance.

(The Changing domestic priorities series)
Includes bibliographical references.
1. Housing—United States—Finance. 2. Mortgage loans—United States. I. Goodman, John L. II. Title. III. Series.
HD7293.Z9T83 1983 332.7'22'0973 83-21757
ISBN 0-87766-328-9

Printed in the United States of America

THE URBAN INSTITUTE is a nonprofit policy research and educational organization established in Washington, D.C. in 1968. Its staff investigates the social and economic problems confronting the nation and government policies and programs designed to alleviate such problems. The Institute disseminates significant findings of its research through the publications program of its Press. The Institute has two goals for work in each of its research areas: to help shape thinking about societal problems and efforts to solve them, and to improve government decisions and performance by providing better information and analytic tools.

Through work that ranges from broad conceptual studies to administrative and technical assistance, Institute researchers contribute to the stock of knowledge available to public officials and to private individuals and groups concerned with formulating and implementing more efficient and effective government policy.

Conclusions or opinions expressed in Institute publications are those of the authors and do not necessarily reflect the views of other staff members, officers or trustees of the Institute, or of any organizations which provide financial support to the Institute.

Advisory Board of the
Changing Domestic Priorities Project

CONTENTS

TABLES

FIGURES

FOREWORD

This report is part of the Changing Domestic Priorities project of The Urban Institute. This project is examining shifts that are occurring in the nation's economic and social policies under the Reagan administration and analyzing the effects of these changes on people, places, and institutions.

The primary aim of the Reagan program in the area of housing finance is one that the administration is pursuing in many other areas, that is, the administration is seeking to reduce the role of the federal government in the processes of the market economy. In the area of housing finance, that entails making an effort to increase the strength of the purely private aspects of a system that was created and has been maintained by the central government. Doing so presents a delicate policy problem as the maintenance of a stable flow of funds to housing is a matter of concern to national economic policy. The abrupt removal of federal structures and supports could be potentially disastrous. In fact, the Reagan approach to housing finance has been an attempt to balance the aims of removing federal intrusion, strengthening private organizations, and maintaining an adequate and stable flow of funds to housing finance.

Deregulation of the housing finance industry began well before the Reagan administration took office. The regulated housing finance system that was set up during the New Deal cracked badly under the strain of high and erratic inflation and interest rates that characterized the U.S. economy in the middle and late seventies. Market participants, regulators, and legislators all attempted to repair the system, but what emerged as the result of their efforts was actually a new system, based on a set of more diversified and lightly regulated primary lenders, and a strong secondary market anchored in federally related entities but with significant private involvement.

The Reagan administration has attempted to further the momentum to a new system while implementing its own changes. Through a number of administrative and legislative actions affecting both primary mortgage lending and the secondary market for mortgage-backed securities, the administration has begun to make its mark on the nation's housing finance system.

The authors begin by thoroughly describing the crisis that gripped the housing finance system during the seventies. Then they analyze the resolution of that crisis as accomplished by market evolution and government action. The Reagan administration's record is given mixed marks, with some successes by the administration in achieving its objectives matched by other instances where rhetoric has far exceeded action. The authors conclude that the housing finance system that has resulted from this process of adjustment is an improved one, better able to provide housing credit under changing economic conditions. Housing, however, will no longer be the financial bargain it once was. Although credit for housing will be produced by the new system in amounts adequate to meet demand, the cost of the credit will be more closely linked to borrowing costs incurred by corporations.

John L. Palmer
Isabel V. Sawhill
Editors

Changing Domestic Priorities Series

ACKNOWLEDGMENTS

While chapters 1, 5, and 6 of this book represent recent analysis, the description of the housing finance system in chapters 2, 3, and 4 has been developed over a period of several years by John A. Tuccillo. Chapters 1, 5, and 6 were written jointly by Tuccillo and Jack Goodman. Helpful comments on the work were received from John Weicher and Raymond Struyk. A major debt of gratitude is owed Robert Buckley, whose insightful comments as principal reviewer did much to shape the book's final form. The manuscript was prepared with notable skill and patience by Shirley Pearson and Katherine Guest.

ABOUT THE AUTHORS

John A. Tuccillo is vice president and director of research and economics for the National Council of Savings Institutions. He previously was director of the Housing and Community Development Research Center at The Urban Institute, where he was affiliated from 1979 until 1983. Dr. Tuccillo's research has focused on the impacts of federal credit institutions on housing and the interaction of the tax system and housing investment. He has been a Brookings Fellow at the Department of Housing and Urban Development, a staff member of the President's Commission on Housing, and a consultant to HUD, GAO, the American Bankers Association, Comptroller of the Currency, and the World Bank. He is the author of *Housing and Investment in an Inflationary World*, and a coauthor of *Federal Housing Policy at President Reagan's Midterm*, as well as numerous journal articles.

John L. Goodman, Jr., is an economist with the Board of Governors of the Federal Reserve System. From 1974 through 1983 he was a senior research associate at The Urban Institute, and he has taught at the University of Virginia. His research on housing economics and demography has been published in leading professional journals, including *Public Policy, Economic Inquiry, Urban Affairs Quarterly*, and *The Review of Economics and Statistics*. Dr. Goodman has testified before the Congress of the United States and has served as a consultant to the Department of Housing and Urban Development, the World Bank, and other organizations. He is a member of the Population Advisory Committee to the U.S. Bureau of the Census, and he serves as secretary-treasurer of the Population Association of America.

CHAPTER 1

INTRODUCTION

The housing finance system of the United States is undergoing a period of change on a scale matched only by the activities that surrounded the system's creation in the New Deal. It is probable that we are currently observing the birth of a new system, one that relies far less on a federal presence than did its predecessor. Until quite recently, the system was anchored by specialized housing lenders who were created by federal actions and who operated within the limits prescribed by federal legislation. These primary mortgage lenders were reinforced by a group of federally sponsored secondary market facilities and were supplemented by other private firms (figure 1 displays the funding structure). The flow of funds through the housing finance system originated with household savings purchased by housing finance institutions and resulted in an increase in purchasing power for those who wished to acquire housing. For the most part, the prices that the institutions paid for funds and the rates that they charged to relend those funds were controlled, directly or indirectly, by federal action.

This system worked admirably, from its inception in the early thirties well into the sixties. Americans became the best-housed population in history, at a cost that represented only a fraction of their incomes. The financial institutions that existed throughout this period were regarded as conduits for a high national purpose. Interest rates and prices remained stable and the shackles of federal regulation were barely felt.

Beginning in the mid-1960s, however, an overexpanding economy exposed several fatal weaknesses in the housing finance system. During this period, growing federal deficits and monetary policy

FIGURE 1

SOURCES OF FUNDS FOR HOUSING, 1981

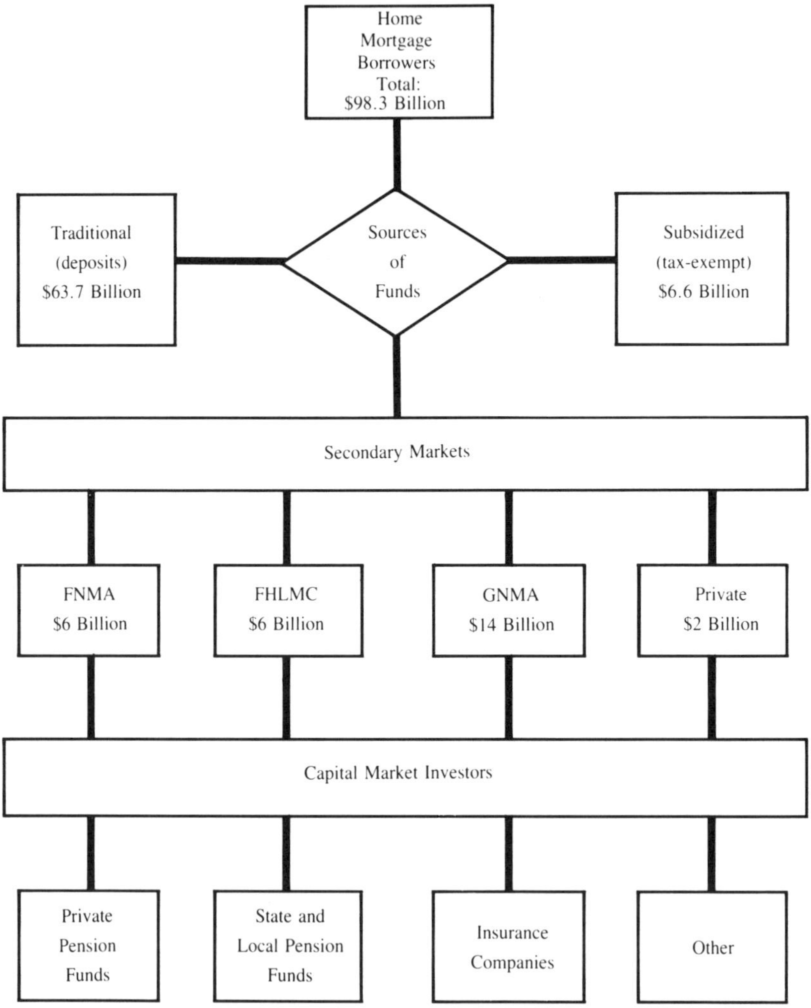

experimentation drove up interest rates and prices, including the prices households were demanding for the use of their savings. This meant that housing lenders needed to bid higher rates, or otherwise face the loss of funds and thus their ability to do business. But because the regulatory structure restricted their ability to raise interest rates, the lenders began to lose funds. Moreover, once rates abated in 1975 and 1976, household savings returned at a much slower rate than they had exhibited prior to the rise. The captive audience was becoming aware of alternatives.

These initial episodes weakened, but did not destroy, the system, because the levels reached by interest and inflation rates were modest.[1] The loss of some funds, however, brought housing lenders to the realization that changes were needed in the instruments at their disposal. As a result of lenders' lobbying, federal regulators made some modest adjustments, with the vague promise of more to come. But when stability seemed to be returning in the early seventies, the system resumed its former ways of doing business. Yet, this time, new elements of competition for funds had been introduced into the system that could not be excised. The more progressive lenders began to see that the past was not to be repeated and began to adjust. Other intermediaries, noting the mobility of household savings, developed new types of instruments that were better tailored to the preferences of savers and were designed to be immune from macroeonomic spasms.

Thus, far from being a cure, the "return to stability" was but a remission. In the mid-1970s, economic volatility resumed and interest rates and inflation rates soared to levels previously unknown in this country. The regulatory structure began to erode. In 1972, the President's Commission on Financial Structure and Regulation, known as the Hunt Commission, had recommended that all depository institutions be granted similar powers and be brought under the same, flexible regulatory umbrella. These suggestions had remained dormant so long as the system behaved. With rising interest rates and the resulting shortage of funds for housing, however, they received more attention. Several financial-reform plans surfaced and worked their way through Congress, only to die because of lack of interest, conflicting goals, or poor design.

The market, however, was not nearly so negligent. As inflation rates rose in 1977 and 1978, unregulated intermediaries, such as money market funds, increasingly attracted household savings. Free of the rate and denomination constraints placed on traditional mortgage lenders, these intermediaries could pass through whatever the market offered as a reward to deposits of virtually any size. For other plans, full financial services were available. But the funds attracted here were no longer available for housing, and without this raw material the old housing finance system cracked and began to break apart.

The years immediately preceding the Reagan administration were a period of extreme stress for the U.S. housing finance system. Inflation raged at record levels; household savings were drained by unregulated institutions; high mortgage rates forced buyers and sellers to deal outside of the intermediary system; and companies like Sears Roebuck and Company and Merrill Lynch Pierce Fenner & Smith established or acquired new mortgage lending facilities. Thus buffeted, savings and loan associations began to disappear through failure or merger in unsurpassed numbers. The system was in trouble and beginning to shatter.

Beneath this tumult, however, a new system was emerging. Beginning in the early 1970s with the financial studies produced by the Hunt Commission and followed by those of the U.S. Federal Reserve System and the House Committee on Banking, Housing and Urban Affairs,[2] a body of analysis was growing that would provide the theoretical and practical guidelines for real reform of the housing finance system. In general, these studies did not take issue with the existing system so much as point out its essential limitations. An analogy may be drawn here with theoretical physics: Einstein did not repeal Newton; he simply pointed out that the Newtonian system was a special case in a more general system of physical laws. Similarly, but more prosaically, analysts pointed out the inflexibility of housing finance in a world of competition and inflation. No set of reform proposals was adopted during the seventies. However, a consensus was developing that there was a right way to approach reform and that lessened reliance on regulation and on a special status for housing finance was the direction to follow.

At the same time, the market reacted to the decline of the official housing finance system by creating a variety of institutions, instruments, and arrangements designed to direct flows of funds to housing. The market reasoned, for example, that if a fixed-rate mortgage in an inflationary world were unattractive to investors, then new types of vehicles that shielded the return on mortgage investment could be developed; furthermore, if money market funds grew and reduced the power of thrifts to attract funds for mortgage investment, the secondary market could be used to liquefy asset holdings and to allow new lending; and if life insurance companies and pension funds were no longer willing to supply funds to housing, private firms would devise new arrangements to fill this gap in the market. Over the course of the seventies, a variety of new instruments were thus introduced, and firms that had previously been strangers to the mortgage market found it profitable to participate. All such instruments were a reaction of the market to the troubles of a highly regulated financial subsystem.

In response to the difficulties experienced by the traditional housing finance institutions and the changes that were occurring in the private market, regulators began to ease the restrictions that had made the system so vulnerable to inflation. While interest rates were still restrained by administered ceilings, new types of accounts were authorized that effectively circumvented existing ceilings and competed with unregulated intermediaries. Similarly, the new mortgage instruments that had been invented by the private market were authorized for regulated institutions. This activity culminated in the Depository Institutions Deregulation and Monetary Control Act (DIDMCA), which went into effect in 1980, the last year of the Carter administration. This law scheduled the end of the deposit interest-rate restrictions and generally freed up the power of regulated institutions to bid for funds against other firms. It thus officially recognized that the old system that had served for almost fifty years was defunct and authorized its replacement by a new, free-market system.

The Reagan Approach

In its early years, the Reagan administration enunciated a program of housing finance measures designed to continue the momentum established by the events of the 1970s. Since the deregulation of the financial market and the fostering of private activity were in philosophic harmony with the Reagan program, this task was gladly accepted. The administration attempted to advance the birth of a new system in three ways. First, the policy body charged with implementing DIDMCA, the Depository Institutions Deregulation Committee (composed of the heads of the major financial regulatory agencies), moved aggressively to eliminate all restrictions on the liabilities of depository institutions. During 1981 and 1982, this body authorized a variety of new types of accounts with interest rates tied to market rates, including an account that competed directly with money market mutual funds. By mid-1982, the structure of interest rate regulation, scheduled to disappear by 1986, was effectively gone.

Second, the administration introduced a companion piece to DIDMCA, which eventually became the Garn–St. Germain bill, whose purpose was to deregulate the asset side of financial institution portfolios. The passage of this measure was prompted by the dire situation of thrift institutions, but it would have been necessary in any case, since DIDMCA had freed these firms to bid as necessary in order to attract funds but had given them little latitude to seek out profitable investment for these funds. Despite the changes that had occurred in the mortgage instrument, fixed-rate (and therefore risky) mortgages were still the norm. The Garn–St. Germain bill gave these institutions the power to diversity their portfolios, thus enabling them to better withstand the risks that accompany financial intermediation.[3]

Finally, private secondary-market participation was encouraged through other types of regulatory and tax initiatives. Building on recommendations contained in the 1982 report of the President's Commission on Housing,[4] the administration relaxed U.S. Department of Labor rules for pension-fund investment, Securities and Exchange Commission (SEC) registration rules, and Federal Reserve margin requirements. All these rules had acted as structural barriers that reduced private firms' incentives to enter the secondary mortgage market. These changes have already led to the entry of one new private secondary-market entity, the Residential Funding Corporation, and have encouraged similar plans from other private firms. To further this activity, the administration proposed to move the federally related secondary mortgage market firms—the Federal National Mortgage Association (FNMA) and the Federal Home Loan Mortgage Corporation (FHLMC)—into the private sector and to phase the Government National Mortgage Association (GNMA) out of existence. While these last policies have yet to be achieved, they remain on the administration's agenda.

These actions were consistent with what can fairly be listed as the four goals of the Reagan administration in the area of housing finance:

1. Reduction of the federal presence in the housing sector
2. Encouragement of the private sector
3. Expansion of the use of new mortgage instruments
4. Assurance of adequate and affordable credit for housing

Despite the early movement toward these objectives, there has been a gap between the administration's rhetoric and its actions. Yielding to political pressure and to economic conditions, the administration has not pursued some policy actions that would be consistent with its goals. The failure to begin to cast off the federally sponsored secondary market institutions—Fannie Mae and Freddie Mac—is an obvious example.

The administration must accept part of the blame for general economic conditions, which have adversely affected housing. The Reagan fiscal program, which combines large tax cuts with substantial increases in military spending, has caused budget deficits of unprecedented size that in turn have contributed to record-high real-interest rates. These interest rates have hampered the administration's ability to reach the goal of affordable housing credit.

High real-interest rates also have indirectly led to the administration's failure to achieve the first two goals listed above. The federal share of the mortgage market has increased. High real-interest rates have reduced the amount of federally supported or guaranteed mortgage credit, but at the same time, other mortgage credit has dropped further, increasing the federal share. In addition, the high real costs of housing have led to widespread congressional support for the continuation of state and local authority to use the tax-exempt borrowing privilege to provide low-rate mortgage funds. If this legislation passes, as seems likely, the result will be increased future federal involvement in a notoriously inefficient way.

A similar problem occurs with goal number two. The private-sector involvement in the mortgage market is growing at a probably unparalleled rate. But, simultaneously, the FNMA, the largest mortgage investor, has, if anything, increased the government's contingent liability at a faster rate. Once again, the unanticipated jump in interest rates made it impossible to pursue the goal effectively. Because of financial conditions, privatization of the FNMA could not have been achieved without major financial disruptions. The result is that privatization has been delayed and the private sector must compete against subsidized institutions in all but a small share of the market, that is, loans that exceed the limits of the federally related agencies. Moreover, if pending legislation succeeds, the FNMA will be permitted to expand even into this high-priced portion of the market.

The events just described point to the crucial role of interest rates in the future of the housing finance system. The announced objective of the Reagan administration's housing finance program is to establish a system that will attract a continuous and sufficient supply of savings to keep investment costs low, while lessening the special advantage of the housing sector in capital markets. If the housing system achieves this long-term objective, then both the housing sector and the economy as a whole will be strong and able to provide sufficient shelter for a growing population. On the other hand, a return to high inflation rates and high interest rates will severely test this new system and will determine ultimately whether it is flexible enough to succeed where the previous arrangement failed.

Plan of This Volume

The rest of this book expands on the observations made in this first chapter. Chapters 2 through 4 describe the evolution of the old housing finance system, from the authorizing legislation in the thirties to the system's fracture in the seventies; chapter 2 examines the origins of the system; chapter 3 discusses the development of new instruments and arrangements in the face of rising and uncertain inflation; and chapter 4 looks at the growth of the secondary mortgage market. Chapters 5 and 6 examine the actions taken by the Reagan administration to further the development of a new housing finance system, as well as the potential long-term impact of these actions. These two chapters also describe several possible futures for the system and suggest some probable paths.

Readers may wish to use this book selectively. Those familiar with the history described in chapters 2 through 4 may choose to skip directly to chapter 5, which begins with an analysis of housing finance in the first half of the Reagan administration. However, since knowledge of the historical events is essential to an understanding of current developments, it is preferable that the two sections of the book be read in conjunction.

CHAPTER 2

A SHORT POLICY HISTORY OF THE HOUSING FINANCE SYSTEM, 1934–1970

Today's housing finance system[1] is fundamentally a creation of legislative actions taken almost fifty years ago. In the wake of the massive defaults on owner-occupied housing that followed the financial collapse of the late 1920s, the federal government created a group of institutions and instruments designed to shield the housing sector from any similar occurrence. The chief features of this legislation were aimed directly at the faults in the system prior to 1929.

Origins of the System

Major features of the depression-era housing system may be summarized as follows:

1. The creation of a federal agency, the Federal Housing Administration (FHA), equipped to insure lenders against the default of mortgage loans. FHA did much to restore confidence in the mortgage market.[2]
2. The promulgation of a mortgage instrument that was consistent with household budgets. Again, this was the product of FHA, which insured a new type of mortgage: the fixed-interest rate, level-payment, self-amortizing note.[3]
3. New federal support to specialized mortgage lenders. In the early 1930s federal legislation was passed that provided for national charters, deposit insurance, and tax exemption for savings and loan associations and mutual savings banks (thrift

institutions), contingent on their specialization in housing finance.

4. The establishment of a secondary market for mortgages. In order to encourage lenders to commit themselves to the location-specific mortgage loan, the federal government provided for "national mortgage associations." When no private firm elected to become such an entity, the federal government created FNMA to buy mortgages from lenders.

The system functioned well into the 1960s. With a stable price level and tax exemption, savings and loan associations and mutual savings banks found it profitable to specialize in mortgage lending. Discretionary lenders such as life insurance companies and commercial banks absorbed excess demand, thus occupying a significant role in the system. Table 1 depicts the pattern of single-family mortgage holdings that had evolved by the mid-1950s.[4]

During the early postwar period, FHA acted as a market. By the mid-1950s, however, the quantitative importance of FHA in the mortgage market was diminished because an expanding housing sector and growing economy made mortgages attractive investments for private institutions. By the end of 1956 FHA insured only a little over 16 percent of all one-to-four-family housing units, down from over 23 percent (on average) in the later 1930s.[5] Table 2 describes the pattern of FHA activity through the 1960s.[6]

Immediately after World War II, FHA was joined by two new institutional lenders. The first of these, the Veterans Administration (VA), began to guarantee mortgage loans on a larger scale. As a result of legislation passed at the end of the war, certain classes of veterans were entitled to mortgage loans with a low (or no) down payment and low interest rates. The entrance of the VA into the mortgage market provided a great incentive to the housing boom of the 1945–1956 period: total VA-guaranteed mortgage volume reached $28.4 billion by 1956, a figure that represented nearly 30 percent of all one-to-four-family mortgage activity.[7]

The second institutional development of note in the immediate postwar period was the increase in the portion of the mortgage market controlled by mortgage companies. These companies differed from other mortgage market institutions in that they operated as mortgage brokers rather than as dealers: instead of originating mortgages to hold in their own portfolios, mortgage companies originated mortgages for sale to other investors. Their profits were de-

TABLE 1

YEAR-END HOLDINGS OF MORTGAGE LOANS ON ONE-TO-FOUR-FAMILY HOMES, BY INVESTOR GROUP, 1950–1956

	Percentage Held by						
Year	*Life Insurance Companies*	*Mutual Savings Banks*	*Savings and Loan Associations*	*Commercial Banks*	*Mortgage Companies*	*Federal Agencies*	*Total Mortgages ($ Billions)*
1950	22.7	11.5	36.0	25.4	1.3	3.9	$37.4
1951	24.4	12.2	34.0	23.7	1.0	4.8	43.5
1952	23.6	12.4	35.3	22.6	1.0	5.1	49.9
1953	23.2	13.0	36.9	21.1	0.9	4.9	56.9
1954	23.1	13.7	37.9	20.2	1.1	4.1	65.9
1955	22.7	14.2	38.5	19.4	1.3	3.9	77.9
1956	22.9	14.8	38.7	18.5	1.1	4.0	87.8

SOURCE: U.S. Department of Housing and Urban Development, *Mortgage Loan Gross Flows* (Washington, D.C.: U.S. Government Printing Office [GPO]), table 19.

TABLE 2

PRIVATELY OWNED HOUSING UNITS STARTED UNDER FHA MORTGAGE-INSURANCE PROGRAMS, COMPARED WITH TOTAL FOR UNITED STATES, 1935–1969
(Units in Millions)

Years	*Total U.S. Units*	*Total FHA Units*	*FHA Units as Percentage of Total U.S. Units*
1935–1939	1.710	.400	23.4
1940–1944	1.773	.806	45.4
1945–1949	5.379	.997	18.5
1950–1954	7.708	1.558	20.2
1955–1959	6.936	1.262	18.2
1960–1964	7.160	1.190	16.2
1965–1969	6.904	.988	14.3

SOURCE: U.S. Department of Housing and Urban Development, *HUD Statistical Yearbook* (Washington, D.C.: GPO, 1978), p. 65.

rived from fees charged for originating the mortgage and servicing it for the ultimate investor. Mortgage companies added two dimensions to the mortgage market. First, by utilizing FHA-insured mortgages, an instrument of diminishing importance to other lenders, mortgage bankers expanded the range of financing terms available to the prospective home purchaser. The growth of mortgage companies provided easier access to FHA mortgages for the borrower. Second, on the other side of the market, the activities of mortgage brokers made it easier for a variety of institutions, especially life insurance companies, to invest in mortgages. The existence of mortgage companies allowed life insurance companies to buy origination and servicing, rather than providing these functions themselves; thus the cost of acquiring mortgages was reduced and mortgage investment was made more attractive.[8]

The System Unravels: 1960–1970

Into the 1960s, the housing finance system that had been formed by the 1930s legislation served the housing sector well: between 1945 and 1965, 27.2 million units were financed and constructed. By the early 1960s, however, the system began to change in a manner that made it more vulnerable to economic swings. The first element of this change was the abandonment of the mortgage market (at least of the one-to-four-family market) by discretionary investors. This was most readily apparent for life insurance companies. In 1950, life insurance companies held 22.7 percent of all outstanding one-to-four-family mortgages. By 1966, this share had fallen to 14.9 percent, and the decline continued into the 1970s.

A similar, and equally dramatic, shift occurred in commerical bank holdings of mortgages. From a 25.4 percent share of the single-family mortgage market in 1950, commercial banks dropped to a 16.1 percent share in 1966. More importantly, bank holdings of mortgages became much more cyclical, expanding at the trough of interest rate cycles and declining at the peak. These changes increased the role of thrift institutions in the housing finance system: the share of total one-to-four-family mortgages held by savings and loan associations rose from 38.5 percent in 1955 to 47.9 percent in 1966; for mutual savings banks, the share rose from 14.2 to 15.3 percent.

The reasons for these shifts are complex, but in the years prior to 1966, the primary reason appears to have been a shift in relative rates of return on mortgages and other securities. Figure 2 shows the spread between mortgage rates and corporate bond rates between 1961 and 1980. This spread fell steadily through the sixties.[9] Because mortgages were refinanced more frequently than corporate securities and thus entailed higher transactions costs for investors over a given holding period, the net return to mortgages was smaller than that on similar corporate securities.

After 1966, the combination of inflation, economic fluctuations, and government regulation significantly reduced the efficiency of the housing finance system: the overexpansion of the economy in the mid-1960s by government fiscal policy generated a continuing rise in the level of prices; increases in the rate of inflation brought on a tight money policy by the Federal Reserve, causing short-term interest rates to rise relative to long-term rates; and the thrift institutions found themselves in the position of buying money at prices higher than expected to finance a portfolio of low-rate mortgages issued in the past. Lender forecasts had proven false, and the resulting uncertainty increased the perceived risk of financing housing.[10]

Typically, such a dilemma is most readily solved by withdrawing from the business of mortgage lending. In fact, this is precisely what commercial banks (and, to a lesser extent, mutual savings

FIGURE 2

INTEREST RATE SPREAD BETWEEN MORTGAGES AND CORPORATE BONDS, 1961–1980

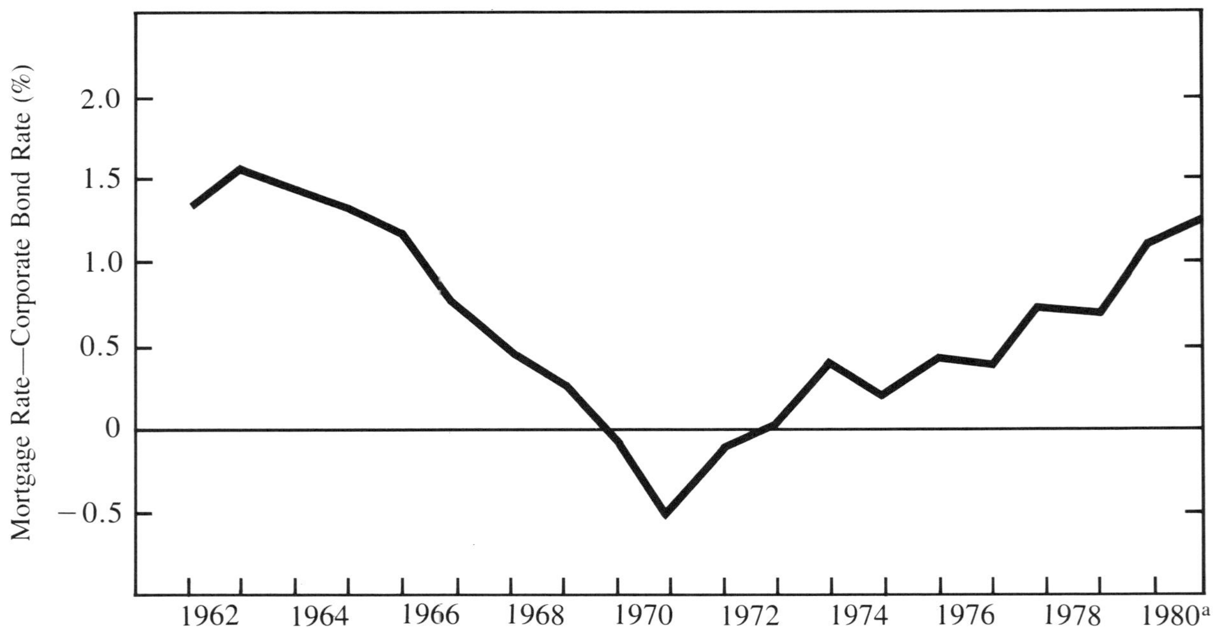

SOURCE: The corporate bond rate is the average of the weekly Aa new-issue reoffering yield, from U.S. Treasury Department, *Treasury Bulletin*, table AY-1. The mortgage rate is the FHA series on new homes, from U.S. Federal Reserve System, *Federal Reserve Bulletin*, various issues.

a. First ten months of 1980.

banks) did during the period. Since the mid-1960s, commercial-bank mortgage lending has been heaviest in those periods when mortgage rates have been sufficiently high to insure the long-term profitability of mortgage lending. Table 3 illustrates the relationship between conventional mortgage rates and the portion of commercial banks' asset flows devoted to mortgage lending from 1963 to 1980. The generally positive relationship between these two indicators during this time period typifies the reaction of lenders that have other outlets for flow of deposit funds. By 1970, the commercial bank share of home mortgages had shrunk to 14.2 percent; mutual savings banks held about 14.1 percent of all home mortgages. Such flexibility, however, was not available to savings and loan associations. Locked into mortgage investment by regulation and tax law,[11] these institutions confronted the prospect of declining profits or shrinking portfolios because of increasing uncertainty about interest rates.

TABLE 3

COMMERCIAL-BANK MORTGAGE ACQUISITIONS AND MORTGAGE RATES, 1963–1980

Year	*Commercial Bank Mortgage Flows as Percentage of Total Asset Acquisition*	*Mortgage Yield in Primary Market (FHLBB[a] Series)*
1963	27.1	5.93
1964	18.3	5.86
1965	18.8	5.81
1966	22.7	6.25
1967	11.2	6.46
1968	15.1	6.97
1969	38.7	7.81
1970	5.4	8.44
1971	17.0	7.74
1972	21.7	7.60
1973	22.2	7.95
1974	17.3	8.92
1975	11.2	9.01
1976	13.6	9.08
1977	19.1	9.02
1978	15.5	9.56
1979	14.9	10.87
1980	10.4	12.86

SOURCES: U.S. Federal Reserve System, *Federal Reserve Bulletin,* various issues.

a. FHLBB = Federal Home Loan Bank Board.

Help for mortgage lenders ostensibly came in the form of federal regulation of deposit rates. In 1966, the Interest Rate Stabilization Act extended the ceiling on commercial bank deposit rates to thrift institutions. This regulatory change was intended to hold down the costs of funds for thrifts and thus ensure the steady flow of funds into housing finance at reasonable rates. If the funds attracted by thrifts were interest inelastic, the implementation of maximum interest rates on deposits would reduce costs without reducing deposit flows.

To provide a competitive edge for savings and loan associations, the ceiling rate on their deposits was set 0.5 percent higher than that of commercial banks. The change came at a time when the rates on all financial assets were rising above previous norms, and the cap on the rates offered by thrifts put them at a severe competitive disadvantage relative to unregulated seekers of funds. Table 4 indicates the extent of this disadvantage. Comparing only those years of relative interest-rate peaks, the share of household savings flowing to savings and loans dropped dramatically after the imposition of the interest rate ceiling. Nor was this a temporary problem. Once lost, these funds rarely found their way back, because households had gained familiarity with a broader variety of market instruments. The interest rate controls not only drained funds out of the housing finance system but also increased the interest sensitivity of the remaining funds.

Thrift institutions also suffered relative to commercial banks. Table 5 indicates the share of household deposits attracted by commercial banks, savings and loans, mutual savings banks, and credit unions. With the extension of interest rate controls, the share of

TABLE 4

SHARE OF HOUSEHOLD SAVINGS GOING TO SAVINGS AND LOAN ASSOCIATIONS IN YEARS OF INTEREST-RATE PEAKS

Year	*Savings and Loan Share*
1955	0.29
1959	0.30
1966	0.11
1969	0.10
1974	0.17

SOURCE: U.S. Board of Governors of the Federal Reserve System, *Flow of Funds Accounts, 1946–1975.*

TABLE 5

DISTRIBUTION OF HOUSEHOLD SAVINGS DEPOSITS, 1951–1980
(Net of Certificates of Deposit)

	Percentage of Deposits Going to			
Year	*Commercial Banks*	*Savings and Loan Associations*	*Mutual Savings Banks*	*Credit Unions*
1951–1955	29	46	21	4
1956–1960	31	51	14	4
1961–1965	43	40	13	4
1966–1970	52	28	15	5
1971–1975	44	40	11	5
1976–1980	43	43	8	6

SOURCE: U.S. Board of Governors of the Federal Reserve System, *Flow of Funds Accounts, 1946–1975.*

savings and loans fell off sharply, from 40 percent of deposits in 1961–1965 to 28 percent in 1966–1970. This decrease reflects the greater flexibility of the other institutions in offering a wide range of deposit instruments.

Nor did the interest rate ceilings reduce thrift costs. The inability to compete with other intermediaries on a price basis led to an emphasis on nonprice competition. Larger offices, more branches, longer hours, and home-appliance giveaways were used by thrifts to attract customers, but at the same time, these measures raised the cost of doing business. A recent study of mutual savings banks indicates that these nonprice competitive actions raised costs by 10 percent to 11 percent of total costs. This would be equivalent to an increase in deposit rates of over 0.5 percent.[12] Savings and loans regained their market share only after they began offering longer-term, high-yield deposits in the early 1970s.

Housing Cycles and Economic Activity

Because housing is traditionally financed over a long term and because the purchase of a house is a consumption decision that can be deferred, the housing sector has exhibited marked cyclical behavior. Between the end of World War II and 1980, the U.S. economy underwent six major housing cycles. Each of the cycles (with the exception of that in 1960–1961) occurred after the implementation of a tight monetary policy and preceded a general downturn in economic activity. The initiating mechanism has been the diversion of loanable funds from housing to other sectors of the economy as deposit rates have fallen relative to the rates on other financial instruments and the supply of funds to mortgage lenders has declined.[13] Figure 3 shows the pattern of housing cycles and identifies periods of recession in general economic activity.[14]

Of greater interest than the cyclic pattern of housing starts is the amplitude of each of the postwar cycles. It appears from figure 3 that the cycles that occurred after the events of the mid-1960s—increased interest rate uncertainty, increased inflation, and deposit rate ceiling—were of greater amplitude than the cycles preceding those changes. Statistics for this time period indicate that this is in fact the case. Table 6 shows the peak-to-trough and trough-to-peak percentage changes of housing starts for postwar cycles to 1980.[15] The recent cycles exhibit both larger declines and larger recoveries than did the pre-1966 cycles.

FIGURE 3

CYCLE OF HOUSING STARTS PRIOR TO RECESSIONS

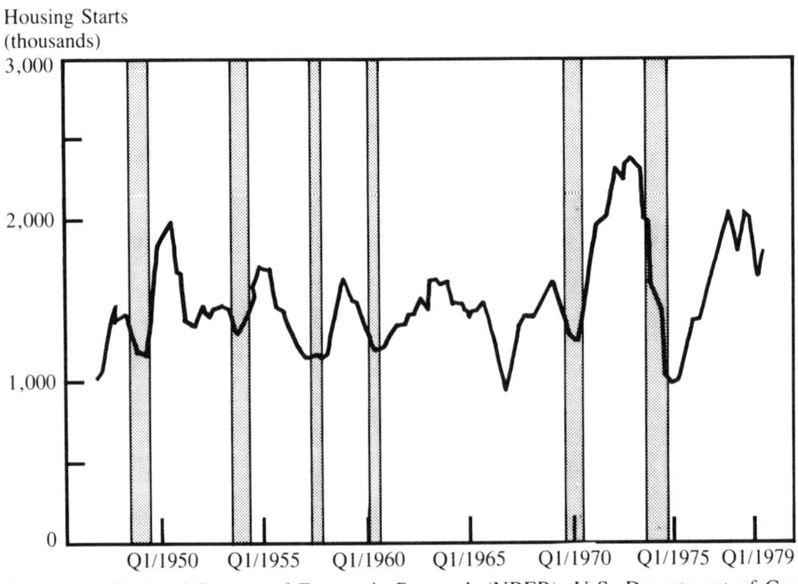

SOURCES: National Bureau of Economic Research (NBER); U.S. Department of Commerce, Bureau of the Census, "Housing Starts," *Construction Reports*, Series c-20 (Washington, DC.: GPO), various issues.

NOTE: Shading indicates recession periods identified by NBER.

TABLE 6

AMPLITUDE OF HOUSING CYCLES, 1947–1980

Cycle Dates[a]	*Percentage Change in Housing Starts, Peak to Trough*	*Percentage Change in Housing Starts, Trough to Peak*
May 1947–April 1951	0.438	0.641
April 1951–October 1956	.377	.288
December 1957–November 1966	.736	.457
July 1967–June 1970	.561	.342
June 1970–December 1974	.936	.783
December 1974–May 1980	0.797	0.837

SOURCE: U.S. Department of Commerce, Bureau of the Census, "Housing Starts," *Construction Reports*, series c-20 (Washington, D.C.: GPO).

a. Trough-to-trough dates.

Summary

The housing finance system that operated with success in this country from the thirties through the sixties was the product of a series of depression-era laws aimed at providing a steady flow of funds to the housing sector. The system's institutions and instruments were designed to operate in a climate of relative price stability and to provide a constant flow of funds whenever interest rates were sufficiently predictable to allow long-range planning.

During the boom housing years of the late 1940s and early 1950s, the system functioned successfully. In the 1960s it began to falter, however. The first factor contributing to the system's malfunction was the narrowing of the market base because of the abandonment of the residential mortgage market by life insurance companies. Lured by higher rates on other securities, these companies shifted their portfolios toward corporate securities and nonresidential real-estate investment. This was a significant loss to the system but was offset partially by the concurrent growth of mortgage bankers as financers of residential investment.

However, the real blow to the system occurred in the mid-1960s as increasing government expenditures and stringent monetary policies drove up the rate of inflation and increased the variability of interest rates. The resulting uncertainty about the future course of economic events placed a squeeze on major mortgage lenders and made it increasingly difficult for them to provide efficient housing-market intermediation. The remedy chosen by public policymakers was the imposition of controls on the prices paid by these institutions for deposits. It was hoped that this would reduce the uncertainty and cost of mortgage lending and thus insure the flow of funds into housing.

The attempted remedy, however, only intensified the problems. Unable to compete either with other depository intermediaries or with the unregulated sector of the financial market, thrift institutions suffered higher costs, owing to the need to rely on nonprice competition to attract deposits. This meant both a deterioration in the competitive position of the major mortgage lenders and an increased reliance on discretionary lenders for housing finance. But institutions—like commercial banks, life insurance companies and pension funds—acquire mortgages when the rate becomes attractive. Since mortgage rates historically have moved less than other interest rates, this means these investors supply mortgage funds sporadically. All of these factors translated into increased instability in the housing sector and greater cyclical swings in housing activity.

This was essentially the position of the housing finance system by the late 1960s. It was clear that there were problems in the system and that reform was necessary. In 1969 that perceived need resulted in the appointment of a presidential commission called the Hunt Commission, aimed at fashioning a new housing finance system.[16] While the commission was ultimately unsuccessful in its attempt, its findings instigated a public awareness that the housing finance system was losing efficiency because it was overregulated and lacked the flexibility to deal with a rapidly changing financial environment.

In the end, it was the pressure of high and erratic interest rates, not the organized reform effort, that generated change. The response to these pressures took the form primarily of the invention by the financial system of new business arrangements that evaded existing regulation and enabled funds to be channeled to the highest-yielding uses. This marked a significant change for the housing sector. Formerly, funds might or might not have been available, but if they were available, the price was lower than it would have been in a free market. Now, under the new system, funds are available if one is willing to pay the market price. The adjustment of the housing finance system to the new rules of the game is a large part of the story of the past decade.

CHAPTER 3

INFLATION, INSTITUTIONS, AND INSTRUMENTS, 1970–1980

As we have seen, significant portions of the housing finance system began to erode in the late 1960s as inflation and interest rate fluctuations drove discretionary investors out of the mortgage market and exerted a profit squeeze on thrift institutions. The persistence of inflation in the early 1970s intensified these trends. But continuing inflation also prompted innovation in other markets: depository institutions invented new instruments that allowed them both to circumvent interest rate ceilings and to attract funds in direct competition with unregulated intermediaries; state and local governments used their tax-exempt borrowing power to gather pools of funds earmarked for subsidized lending; and lenders introduced new mortgage instruments aimed at overcoming inflation-induced barriers to mortgage lending.

This chapter looks at the influence of continuing high inflation rates on the housing finance system and also describes the effect of the introduction of new deposit and mortgage instruments by both public and private agents. Each of these factors contributed substantially to the changes in the housing system that occurred in the 1970s.

The Impact of Inflation on Housing and Housing Finance

Ironically, while high and variable rates of inflation make mortgage lending a risky and somewhat unattractive proposition, they also increase the demand for housing investment and, therefore, the demand for housing finance. This was especially true in the 1970s, when demographic changes, tax laws, and other factors combined to guarantee that housing prices rose faster than the general rate of inflation. As the rate of increase in the Consumer Price Index jumped from a 6.1 percent average annual rate in the 1970–1974 period to an 8.6 percent average in the 1974–1979 period, prices climbed at a 9.4 percent rate, for the constant quality house.[1] The relatively high rate of growth of housing prices was accompanied by high levels of home sales, with the years of the late 1970s having record or near-record sales of new homes.

The impact of inflation on housing is complex, but can be summarized in three propositions:

1. Inflation biases savings away from financial assets and toward real assets; because of tax treatment and accessibility, owner-occupied housing is a preferred real asset for households in periods of inflation.
2. Inflation pushes nominal interest rates up and increases the outlays required to maintain homeownership.
3. Inflation, combined with the standard mortgage instrument and the tax system, reduces the real cost of acquiring housing.

The proposition that a fixed-return asset is unattractive in periods of rapid inflation is reasonably intuitive. A financial asset is essentially a promise to pay or to receive a given amount of money at the end of a given time period. The greater the rate of increase in prices during the time period, the lower will be the purchasing power of the return flow of funds. In periods of high inflation, interest rates rise, so that lenders will receive a nominal return that offsets the erosion of purchasing power by the increase in prices over time.[2]

The inflation bias against fixed-return assets is even more severe if the rates of return on those assets do not incorporate an inflation premium. Perhaps the most striking examples of this situation are the deposits of regulated financial institutions. As the rate of inflation increases, and as market interest rates rise to compensate, regulated institutions must retain administratively constrained rates. Adjustments in these rates generally lag the market, do not fully reflect inflation, and therefore result in movements out of regulated instruments when market rates rise. This is the disintermediation process that was associated with sharp increases in interest rates and inflation in 1966, 1969, 1974, and 1979. During these periods, funds flowed out of the major mortgage lenders into unregulated instruments.[3] The share of total household savings flowing to regulated depository institutions fell from 56 percent in 1966 to 33 percent in 1969 and had returned to only 47 percent by 1974.[4]

Within depository institutions themselves, inflation altered the composition of deposits. As the unregulated sector of the financial market presented more severe competition, regulated institutions began to invent instruments to the extent possible within regulatory bounds.[5] The result of this was the gradual decline of the lowest rate instrument, the regular passbook account. In 1970, for example, these accounts comprised 53 percent of the total savings and loan association deposit volume. By the end of 1980, this percentage had shrunk to 21 percent.[6]

In terms of the housing finance system, the decline in the portion of savings flowing into regulated institutions can lead either to a decline in the funds available for mortgages or to an increase in the rate on mortgages. At different times, both effects have been observed, but the interest rate effect is most likely to predominate. Essentially, mortgage lenders will replace lost savings funds through more costly borrowings. The flow of funds to mortgage finance will continue but will reflect the higher cost of funds to lending institutions. Figure 4 describes the relationship between the cost of funds to savings and loans and mortgage rates from the mid-sixties to the early eighties.

These higher costs of funds are, in turn, translated into higher mortgage rates (our second proposition), which affect the payment burden of the household entering the housing market. Taken together, rising house prices and rising mortgage rates mean that the home buyer (especially the home buyer who is unable to tap equity from a previous house) needs to commit a substantial portion of income to homeownership costs. By conventional rule of thumb, the average household should devote no more than about 25 percent of its income to housing expenses. As the carrying costs for housing have risen, however, the percentage of U.S. households able to maintain the median-priced new house by an expenditure of only 25 percent of their income has declined. Table 7 illustrates the trend in this ratio under the assumption of a 25 percent down payment.

Basically, these figures document the combined effects of rising inflation in the costs of producing houses, increased maintenance

FIGURE 4

SPREAD BETWEEN INTEREST RETURN ON MORTGAGES HELD AND AVERAGE COST OF FUNDS TO FSLIC-INSURED SAVINGS AND LOANS

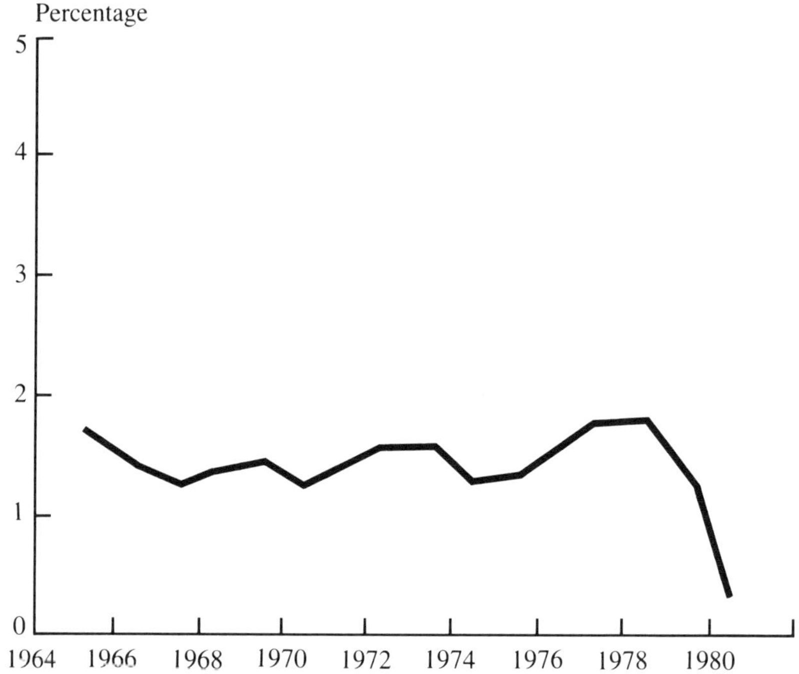

SOURCE: "Statistical Series," tables 5.4.8 and 5.4.11, *Federal Home Loan Bank Board Journal*, vol. 14, no. 5 (May 1981), pp. 69–70, and earlier issues.

and utilities costs, and higher mortgage rates generated by inflation. To the extent that these figures reflect rising current outlays necessary for homeownership, they tell only a part of the story, however. The figures do not take into account the fact that in relative terms, mortgage rates in the late seventies were still a bargain, and that the true cost of homeownership was low[7] and, possibly, negative (proposition number three).[8]

The result of the long- and short-run advantages of housing investment was a steadily rising ratio of new mortgage debt to the value of the net residential investment. In the 1961–1970 period,

TABLE 7

PERCENTAGE OF FAMILIES IN THE UNITED STATES ABLE TO AFFORD NEW HOMES, 1967–1978

Year	*HUD Series*[a]	*Census Series*[b]
1967	41.2	34.7
1968	37.6	28.7
1969	38.3	32.3
1970	45.2	31.7
1971	44.0	32.4
1972	42.8	33.0
1973	36.8	31.3
1974	31.4	25.7
1975	31.5	23.7
1976	27.2	22.7
1977	34.4	—
1978	29.1	—

SOURCES: John G. Weicher, "New Home Affordability, Equity, and Housing Market Behavior," *AREUEA Journal,* vol. 6, no. 4 (winter 1978), exhibit 1, p. 398. Figures for 1977 and 1978 calculated by John A. Tuccillo.

NOTE: Table is based upon the assumption of a 25 percent down payment.

a. Calculated from U.S. Department of Housing and Urban Development, *1976 Statistical Yearbook* (Washington, D.C.: GPO, 1978), p. 238.

b. Calculated from U.S. Department of Commerce, Bureau of the Census, "Prices of New One-Family Homes Sold," *Construction Reports,* series C-27.

this ratio was 1.26:1, increasing to 1.56:1 for 1971–1974, and to 1.76:1 for 1975–1978.[9] This means that in 1978, homeowners were capitalizing net residential investment more than one and three-quarter times over. This is symptomatic of the capital gains available in housing and represents a potentially procyclical reservoir of purchasing power in an inflationary economy.

Changes in Deposit Instruments

During the seventies, the range and nature of deposit instruments offered by major mortgage lenders changed significantly, owing to the fact that regulated interest rates combined with persistent inflation nullified any positive real return to these accounts.[10] The reluctance of households to place their savings in negative-yield instruments led to the development of consumer-oriented savings vehicles by the unregulated sector of the financial system, and to an attempt by the regulated sector to circumvent interest rate controls. Activities on the part of the regulated intermediaries have been focused both on transactions accounts and on savings deposits as thrift institutions have attempted to compete with the unregulated sector as well as with commercial banks.

The invention of negotiable order of withdrawal (NOW) accounts in New England in the early seventies represented the first significant challenge by thrifts of the commerical bank monopoly on household *transactions* accounts.[11] Since NOWs serve as checking accounts and pay interest, they tended to dominate conventional checking accounts.

The first major crack in the system of regulated savings instruments offered by the major mortgage lenders occurred in 1973, when the Federal Reserve, reacting to the sharp run of interest rates followed by a severe disintermediation, suspended interest rate ceilings on longer-term consumer certificates of deposits, quickly attracting $27 billion in funds to intermediaries. Unfortunately, financial regulators backed away from this experiment after two weeks.[12]

With the recurrence of sharply rising rates and disintermediation in 1977–1978, regulatory authorities once again moved to restore the competitiveness of intermediaries, this time within the framework of deposit rate regulation. In July 1978, the Federal Reserve and the Federal Home Loan Bank Board (FHLBB) authorized two new savings instruments. The first of these, a long-term certificate that bore a maximum interest rate of 8 percent, never really proved popular with savers; interest rate expectations were such that an 8 percent return was significantly below long-term market rates.

The second instrument, the money market certificate (MMC), had a significant impact on the flow of funds through mortgage lenders. MMCs are six-month, low-denomination certificates that carry an interest rate linked to the rate on U.S. Treasury Department bills (T-bills).[13] The impact of the MMC on the housing finance system is typified by the disintermediation period of 1978, when deposit flows to financial intermediaries were actually negative to all categories except for the MMC. By the end of 1980, MMCs accounted for 36 percent of all savings and loan deposits.

In 1979, following the success of the MMC, regulatory authorities introduced a longer-term (30 months), lower-denomination certificate that also mirrored T-bill rate movements. Both these instruments were vehicles for the gradual deregulation of deposit interest rates, and as such, have allowed financial intermediaries to compete with unregulated institutions for household savings. For the housing finance system, the effects of this enhanced flexibility have been twofold. First, the flow of funds into housing has tended to stabilize. With thrifts able to compete with other intermediaries for funds on an interest rate basis, there has been virtually no period when the funds available for mortgages have dried up because they were bid away to other purposes. Second, the ability to compete has meant that mortgage lenders have sustained higher costs of funds, thus affecting the terms offered in the mortgage market. If the flow of funds to mortgages becomes more stable, it will become so only at a higher price and probably only through instruments currently unfamiliar to the major institutions in the mortgage market.

Alternative Mortgage Instruments

A second response to persistent inflation during the seventies was the interest on the part of both borrowers and lenders in alternatives to the standard mortgage instruments. On the borrower side, the increase in payment burden generated by high mortgage rates and high housing prices prompted a search for an instrument that would lower the cash flow necessary to achieve homeownership. Lenders, on the other hand, desired a mortgage instrument whose return was indexed to inflation. Such an instrument would ease the profit squeeze connected with the financing of a long-term, fixed-rate asset portfolio by offering a short-term, variable-rate liability portfolio during periods of high and uncertain inflation. Both these desires are symptomatic of the weaknesses of the fixed-rate mortgage during inflation, as described in the following paragraphs.

Since the standard mortgage contract calls for a fixed interest rate and fixed payments throughout its terms, lenders need to build in a compensation for expected inflation. If this factor is accurately estimated, the total payments in real terms associated with any mortgage are the same regardless of the rate of inflation. However, the nominal payments made on a mortgage are highly sensitive to the rate of inflation: the higher the rate of inflation, the higher the nominal mortgage payment. Thus, in the early years of a mortgage issued during a period of price inflation, the fixed nominal payment is higher in real terms than in later years because the price level is lower. If there were no inflation and the price level remained unchanged, both real and nominal payments would be constant over the entire term of the mortgage. Put another way, at higher rates of inflation, real payments will be higher in the early years of the mortgage than at lower rates of inflation, displaying what is known as a "tilt."[14] Figure 5 displays both these effects and shows the pattern of real mortgage payments at different rates of inflation over the life of the mortgage. Note that for each of these real payment streams, there is a corresponding *constant* nominal payment stream.

Essentially what has happened is that the shortcomings of the standard mortgage instrument, designed for a period of low and constant inflation, have been exposed by a long period of high and fluctuating inflation rates. The need for a substitute has centered on the need of both borrowers and lenders to have mortgage payments indexed. For borrowers, this means the indexing of payment

FIGURE 5

REAL VALUE OF MONTHLY PAYMENTS

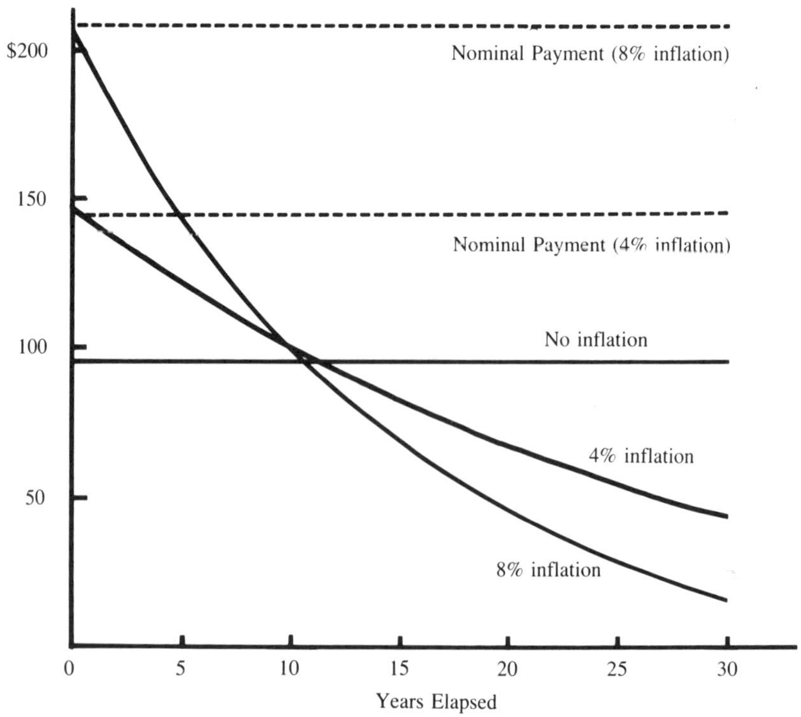

to rising income; for lenders, it means the indexing of mortgage interest rates to market rates. Although the two major alternatives to the standard mortgage that have been implemented to date address these indexing needs, neither alternative satisfies both borrowers and lenders.[15]

The earliest alternative to the standard mortgage to be implemented on any large scale was the variable-rate mortgage (VRM). This instrument differs from the standard mortgage in that it carries an interest rate that changes with market rates; thus, the payment made by the mortgage varies with the rate prevailing on the mortgage.[16] The intent of the VRM is to allow the return on the mortgage portfolio of the lender to rise and fall as market rates change. In effect, the VRM changes a long-term mortgage portfolio into the equivalent of a portfolio of short-term assets.

The VRM also relieves the lender of the uncertainty associated with future interest rates. By allowing the mortgage rate to shadow the market automatically, the lender need not predict future rates. The burden of uncertainty still remains but is transferred to the borrower, who must determine whether he or she can sustain the possibility of higher payments generated by future interest rates.

This transfer of risk is precisely what makes VRMs unattractive to borrowers. The fact that the portfolios of households are smaller and less diversified than those of financial intermediaries makes them less efficient in risk bearing. Thus, consumer groups argue that the transfer of interest rate risk to households is unjustified. This argument shaped the early VRM experiments in the United States.

After 1979, when the Federal Home Loan Bank Board extended VRM authority to federally insured savings and loans, lenders were not particularly eager to offer them, for two reasons. First, mortgage rates were relatively high and were expected to fall. Extension of a fixed-rate loan would lock a high-rate asset into the portfolio for a relatively long time period,[17] while the rate on a VRM loan would automatically fall when rates came down. Although a falling rate could be offset by pricing patterns, lenders were unwilling to alter rates sufficiently, preferring to issue fixed-rate loans. Second, the consumer safeguards attached to VRMs were bothersome and costly to lenders. Particularly troublesome was the requirement that lenders prepare for the borrower's "worst case" examples (loan payment streams for the situation in which the VRM rate rose to its ceiling in the shortest possible time).

The other major alternative to the standard mortgage that emerged during the seventies was the graduated-payment mortgage (GPM). Under the GPM, payments over the life of the mortgage are sufficient to amortize the loan at a fixed interest rate; however, timing of the payments is adjusted so that, compared to the standard instrument, payments in the early years of the loan are lower and those in the later years are higher. Figure 6 indicates the relative payment patterns of both the standard mortgage and GPMs of similar terms. Clearly, the GPM is intended to offset the earlier-described tilt in real payment that results from high rates in inflation. In fact, if the rate of graduation is correctly chosen, the real payment stream of a GPM will resemble that of a standard mortgage in an inflation-free world.

The implementation of GPMs has been accomplished through FHA insurance of these mortgages, which began in 1977 under the Section 245 program. FHA offers mortgages whose payments are graduated over limited periods, either five or ten years. Thus, initial payments do not fall as low (or final payments rise as high) as under an unrestricted GPM.

Mortgages insured under Section 245 quickly became a significant part of FHA business. From a 5.5 percent share of FHA in-

FIGURE 6

MODIFIED GPM PAYMENTS

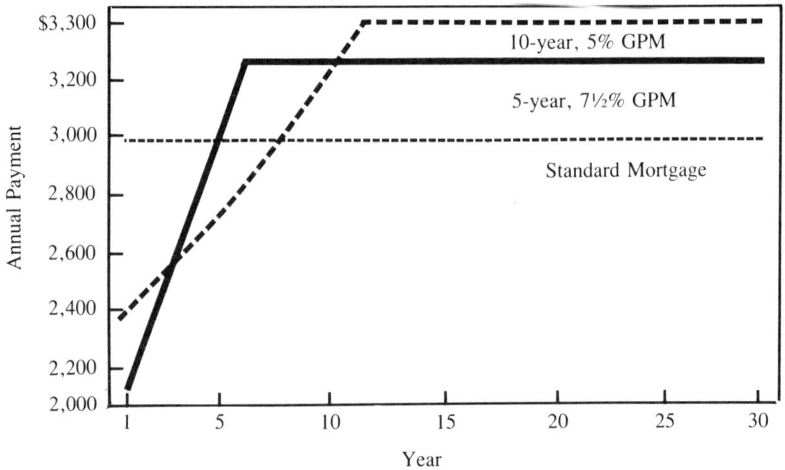

surance in the first quarter of 1978, Section 245 mortgages rose to nearly 30 percent of all FHA activity at the beginning of 1979, and by 1980 represented about 26 percent of all FHA-insured mortgages. By and large, the GPM has accomplished its aims: borrowers under this program are younger and have lower incomes than borrowers under standard FHA programs. It thus appears that the graduated-payment mortgage has, in its limited experience, neutralized the inflation-induced tilt in mortgage payments.[18]

All alternative instruments share a common characteristic in that they are designed to overcome a weakness exhibited by the standard instrument in a period of high and variable inflation. None of the above-described instruments can fully replace the standard instrument, since each is geared to the needs of a particular segment of the mortgage market. Creation of these instruments, however, is a typical reaction of the mortgage market to unrelieved inflation. As such, the instruments represent potentially important factors in the evolution of the housing finance system.

Local Mortgage-Revenue Bonds

The rising outlays necessary to achieve homeownership have prompted local governments to devise ways of subsidizing potential home buyers. The most important of these devices is the local mortgage-revenue bond. Basically, the bond is used to extend the savings from the tax-exempt borrowing privilege of the local government to the home buyer. Bonds are issued and the proceeds from their sale are used to establish a pool of mortgage funds, to be loaned to households that meet certain criteria, at subsidized interest rates. The lower interest rates reduce the income burden of homeownership and thus enable lower-income families to afford housing.

The first local mortgage-revenue bonds were issued by the city of Chicago in mid-1978. At a time when mortgage rates were at about 10 percent, the mortgage-revenue bond allowed the extension of thirty-year mortgages at about 8 percent.[19] From that initial bond issue in the amount of $100 million, the volume of mortgage revenue bonds grew to over $4 billion by mid-1979. By that time, Congress had taken note of the growth of the bonds and had become concerned about the impact of unrestricted mortgage revenue bonds and about the continuing use of the tax-exempt market for private purposes.

Congress, therefore, declared a moratorium on the issuance of mortgage-revenue bonds, pending consideration of several alternative bills to limit their use. After extensive hearings and debates, Congress imposed in December 1980 a limit on the use of mortgage-revenue bonds. The bonds were restricted in amount to 5 percent of the mortgage market in a given locality; the bonds could be used only to finance the purchase of houses up to 110 percent of the median area housing price; and they were limited in the degree of interest rate subsidy. In addition, the law carried a "sunset" provision that prohibited the issuance of mortgage revenue bonds after December 1983.

Mortgage-revenue bonds, by and large, have not been successful in expanding homeownership opportunities. This is because the income limitations for most such bond programs make the vast majority of the population eligible for subsidized loans, and in practice, middle-and upper-income families have availed themselves of the subsidy more than lower-income groups. In a sense, mortgage-revenue bond programs are similar to housing programs such as the GNMA Tandem plan (see note 8). However, the bond programs provide shallower subsidies and are thus less effective at reaching lower-income groups.

Like new deposit and mortgage instruments, local mortgage revenue bonds represent an innovation in housing finance prompted by unchecked inflation. Such bonds are an attractive device to offset the increasingly large cash outlays associated with acquiring a house. Despite their limited effectiveness so far, the bonds have led to the participation by state and local governments as significant mortgage lenders in the housing finance system, a position these governing bodies are likely to retain, regardless of the future of mortgage-revenue bonds.

Summary

Although inflation has increased the real rate of return on housing and thus the demand for housing as an asset, it has been the reaction of housing lenders and federal and local governments to the problem of inflation in housing that has changed the shape of the housing finance system and will continue to determine the future character of the system.

Lenders in the seventies and eighties have chosen to innovate on both sides of their balance sheets in order to continue to attract funds for mortgage lending. On the liability side, they have developed new deposit instruments to compete with unregulated market instruments for households savings. Thrift institutions, for example, have introduced interest-bearing checking accounts and short-term consumer certificates of deposits. Both these devices effectively circumvent federal-interest regulation and allow thrift institutions to offer returns to households that are competitive with other savings vehicles. Such devices have also spurred the development of other liability forms to generate funds for mortgage lending.

On the other side of the balance sheet, private and public experimentation have emphasized alternatives to the standard mortgage instrument. These alternatives were designed to meet specific defects encountered by participants in the mortgage market. The variable-rate mortgage, for example, was crafted to provide the lender with a rate of return to the mortgage portfolio that shadowed market interest rates; and the graduated-payment mortgage was intended to offset the payment "tilt" generated by inflation. Both of these instruments are beginning to make inroads in the monopoly of the standard mortgage; however, neither holds the prospect of becoming a dominant mortgage-lending vehicle.

Finally, local governments have attempted to address the problems created by inflation in the mortgage market through the invention of the mortgage-revenue bond. These bonds were a device that allowed the local government to translate its tax-exempt borrowing privilege into subsidized rate mortgages for middle-and lower-income households. Unfortunately, the result of these programs has been the extension of a subsidy to upper-income households. Although recent congressional action has placed restrictions on the use of the mortgage-revenue bonds, local-government financing of housing appears here to stay.

The changes in the housing finance system that have taken place over the past decade have been the result of problems caused by inflation: when lenders are squeezed, they invent new devices to attract funds; borrowers see the goal of homeownership receding and create pressures that result in new mortgage instruments. The collective result of these changes, however, is a more flexible housing finance system than the one that existed at the beginning of the 1970s. In terms of the savings and mortgage vehicles now available, the housing finance system of 1980 is as unlike the system of 1970 as the system of 1970 differed from that of 1930.

CHAPTER 4

THE DEVELOPMENT OF THE SECONDARY MARKET FOR MORTGAGES

The changes in deposit and mortgage instruments that occurred during the seventies were accompanied by the development of a secondary market for mortgages. Prior to 1968, the general absence of a facility for the selling of mortgage loans restricted the mortgage market to ultimate investors only. Since mortgage loans were location-specific and the nature of the repayment stream uneven, only specialized lenders were comfortable being ultimate investors in mortgages, and the base of the housing finance system remained narrow. This situation stood in sharp contrast to other financial markets, in which instruments traded freely among numerous investors and a well-developed network of dealers created a market in those instruments. Because of the lack of an active secondary market, the mortgage market was segregated from other financial markets.

Over the course of the seventies, this situation changed dramatically. The activities of federally sponsored credit agencies (chiefly GNMA, FNMA, and the FHLMC) and the innovations of private lenders and bond dealers began to tie the mortgage market more closely to other financial markets.[1] The result has been the creation of bond-like vehicles that open the mortgage market to new investors, as well as the provision of a facility for lenders to sell mortgages. This change, together with a national preemption of state usury laws, has generated a fuller integration of mortgages with other capital instruments.

Specifically, three major developments over the 1970–1979 period have set the course of the secondary mortgage market:

1. The growth of the FNMA as a mortgage investor and a guaranteed market for mortgage originators
2. The development by GNMA and FHLMC of methods to package and sell participations in portfolios of whole mortgages
3. The development by the private sector of bond-like instruments collateralized by mortgages and the integration of these instruments into existing financial arrangements

This chapter traces the history of these developments and analyzes their impact on the institutions and instruments of the housing finance system through 1980.

The Growth of FNMA

The Federal National Mortgage Association was founded in 1938 as a vehicle for purchasing federally insured mortgages to smooth out housing cycles and for funneling subsidies to mortgage issuers.[2] In 1968, the subsidy function was split off and the charter amended to turn FNMA into a private corporation with a degree of federal sponsorship and control. From 1968 to 1980, FNMA grew rapidly, its mortgage holdings expanding from $7.2 billion to over $57 billion. FNMA also became more active in the acquisition of conventional mortgages. In 1968, 97 percent of FNMA's net mortgage purchases consisted of FHA-insured and VA-guaranteed mortgages; by the end of the seventies, that figure had fallen to about 50 percent. Table 8 traces this growth. In addition, the share of FHA and VA mortgages in the FNMA portfolio fell from 95 percent in 1973 to 64 percent in 1980.

The majority of FNMA transactions are mortgage purchases. This is unusual since, presumably, FNMA is primarily involved with the stabilization of credit flows to housing. In that case, one would expect that purchases (during periods of credit stringency) and sales (during periods when mortgage credit is relatively easy) would roughly balance out, net of any trends in the total volume of mortgage credit. In practice, however, FNMA has chosen to become a major mortgage investor, so that, in a sense, it is an intermediary between the mortgage market and the bond market. This occurs because FNMA issues debt in the form of corporate securities in order to finance the purchase of mortgages. Furthermore, since FNMA debt tends to be of a higher quality than other corporate debt,[3] it can profitably adopt

TABLE 8

FNMA HOME-MORTGAGE PURCHASES, 1968–1980

Years	*Percentage FHA and VA*	*Percentage Conventional*	*Total Purchases ($ Billions)*
1968	100	a	1.94
1969	100	a	4.12
1970	100	a	2.93
1971	100	a	3.57
1972	97	3	3.70
1973	77	23	6.13
1974	76	24	6.95
1975	85	15	4.26
1976	25	75	3.61
1977	50	50	4.78
1978	54	46	12.30
1979	51	49	10.80
1980	67	33	8.10

SOURCE: Federal National Mortgage Association.

a. No conventional purchase program.

a position of replacing higher-risk debt with lower-risk debt in the financial sector. Both aspects of FNMA operations correspond to the classic definition of intermediary functions.[4]

Until recently, FNMA conducted its transactions through an auction system. Every other week it received bids from mortgage originators wishing to sell mortgages during a given time period. When the bids were received, FNMA decided on the price (mortgage yield) it wished to accept and issued commitments to buy all the mortgages offered at that price or lower; the commitments were valid for a period of up to four months. In addition, it accepted bids that had been made "at the market," that is, bids submitted with no stated price. Separate auctions were conducted for FHA, VA, and conventional mortgages.

The auction-commitment system served FNMA's major customers, the mortgage bankers. Mortgage bankers perform a brokerage function in the mortgage market, in that they originate and service mortgages but sell ownership of the mortgages to other investors. Since the origination process takes time, and since the market for mortgages is traditionally thin, mortgage brokering is risky. FNMA reduced this risk by assuring mortgage bankers a price and a guaranteed market for the mortgage loans they close. If interest rates rose between the time the FNMA commitment was received and the time the broker wished to deliver mortgages, FNMA prevented the mortgage banker from incurring a capital loss. On the other hand, if the average interest rate on mortgages fell, the broker could still sell off the loans to other investors and receive a capital gain on the brokerage operation. This reduction of risk induced mortgage banking operations to expand.[5] Table 9 traces the growth of the percentage of FNMA business accounted for by mortgage bankers and other sellers.

In 1981, FNMA abandoned the auction-commitment system in favor of a fixed-commitment fee system and began offering mandatory as well as optional commitments at lower fee levels. One result of this has been a fourfold increase in commitment fee levels. The full effects of this increase were masked by a relatively desultory mortgage market during 1982, but appear to be significant in a more active market. The most important of these effects is likely to be a further concentration of origination as smaller firms find themselves unable to operate profitably with the higher optional-delivery fees or with the added risk attached to mandatory deliveries.

The previous discussion suggests that FNMA has had a positive impact on the flow of funds into housing. Indeed, if one considers the expansion of mortgage banking activity as a response to the reduction of risk through the FNMA auction, and if one considers that FNMA, through the issue of its debt, is channeling funds from new investors to housing finance, then the conclusion appears valid. Reinforcing this is evidence from a number of empirical studies that FNMA increases mortgage flows in the short run and decreases mortgage rates in the long run.[6] However, evidence also indicates that FNMA has grown at the expense of other suppliers of funds for housing. This trend is apparent in figure 7, which shows mortgage market shares over the past two decades. Of special interest is the relationship between market shares for government agencies (including FNMA) and discretionary investors (particularly life insurance companies and private pension funds) over the 1970–1980 period.

On balance, the emergence of FNMA over the past decade has been a positive element in the housing finance system, since it has provided a guaranteed market for mortgages, at fixed prices, over an extended time period. The stability it has offered has thus reduced the uncertainty attached to mortgage origination and increased the activity of mortgage bankers. Further, as an intermediary between bond and mortgage markets, FNMA has, in effect, introduced new

TABLE 9

TOTAL FNMA PURCHASES BY TYPE OF SELLER, 1969–1980
($ in Millions)

Year	*Total Purchases*	*Percentage Accounted for by*			
		Mortgage Banks	*Savings and Loans*	*Commercial and Mutual Savings Banks*	*Others*[a]
1969	$ 4,120	88.8	1.0	9.1	1.1
1970	2,933	85.0	1.2	12.6	1.2
1971	3,574	83.0	2.0	12.8	2.2
1972	3,699	75.5	3.0	14.2	7.3
1973	6,127	78.4	2.1	12.4	7.1
1974	6,954	81.6	2.0	13.1	3.3
1975	4,262	85.3	2.6	10.2	1.9
1976	3,606	42.5	1.1	6.3	50.1
1977	4,780	88.0	2.1	8.1	1.8
1978	12,303	85.4	6.0	6.2	2.4
1979	10,805	80.7	10.6	7.3	1.4
1980	8,101	80.4	9.3	9.2	1.1

SOURCE: Mortgage Bankers Association of America, Department of Economics and Education.

a. Primarily purchases from Government National Mortgage Association.

FIGURE 7

MORTGAGE MARKET SHARES, 1960–1980

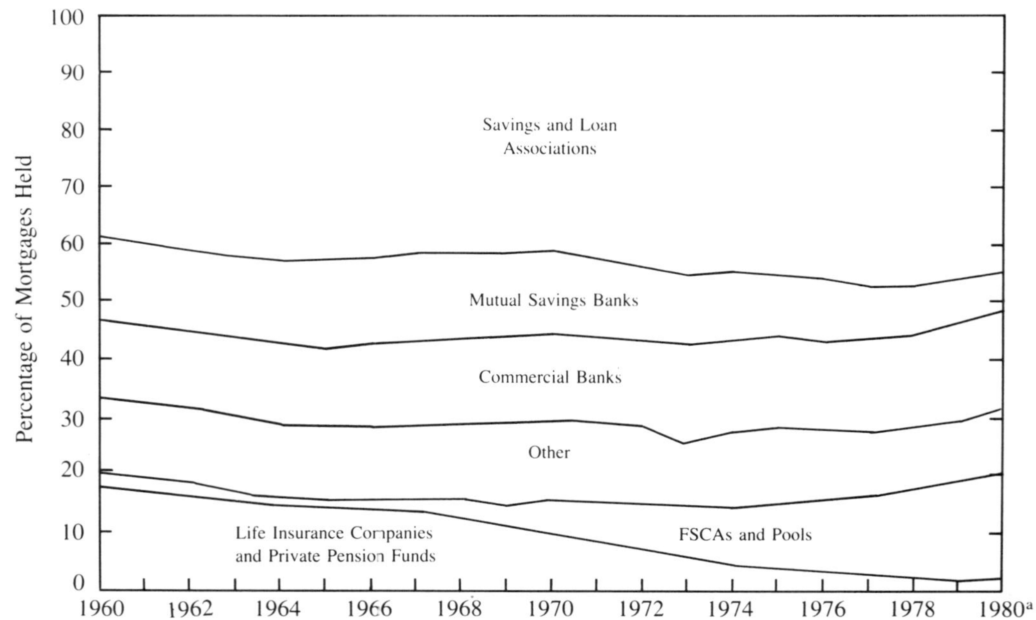

SOURCES: U.S. Board of Governors of the Federal Reserve System, *Flow of Funds Accounts: 1949–1978* (Washington, D.C.: 1979); and *Federal Reserve Bulletin*, various issues.

a. First three quarters of 1980.

sources of funds to mortgage markets. While this activity may have in part merely replaced the mortgage lending of other institutions, it has resulted in a net gain in the supply of mortgage funds.

GNMA, FHLMC, and the Mortgage-Backed Security

When FNMA was made a private corporation in 1968, its special-assistance functions were retained by the government and vested in a new entity, the Government National Mortgage Association (GNMA). As part of its special-assistance functions, GNMA introduced a securities program in 1970 that was aimed at expanding the sources of mortgage credit. Under this program, GNMA would guarantee the timely payment on securities that were collateralized by pools of FHA-insured mortgages. Purchasers of these securities bought an undivided share of the mortgage pool and received a return that reflected the payment of principal and interest on those mortgages. Because these payments are passed through to ultimate investors, the arrangement is known as a pass-through security (PTS). With the PTS, GMNA links mortgage originators with capital market investors, thus helping to integrate mortgage markets into bond markets.

The GNMA pass-through security has proven successful: by the end of 1980, total volume outstanding exceeded $93 billion. Moreover, a large share of these securities was held by investors who were either not traditionally involved with the mortgage market or had reduced their holding of whole mortgage in recent years (e.g., pension funds). Table 10 shows the distribution of pass-through securities by holder for selected years during the seventies.

Following the success of the GNMA pass-through security, FHLMC began issuing similar instruments. These differ from the GNMA securities in that the underlying mortgages are not federally insured, and they are first purchased by FHLMC. FHLMC's pass-through security is called a participation certificate (PC).[7] By the end of 1980, PCs and FHLMC mortgage-backed bonds had grown to an outstanding volume of nearly $17 billion. Again in contrast to GNMA pass throughs, most of these securities were held by financial intermediaries.[8]

TABLE 10

OWNERSHIP OF GNMA PASS-THROUGH SECURITIES, SELECTED YEARS 1971–1980
(Percentage of Outstanding Volume)

	Year							
Investor	*1971*	*1973*	*1974*	*1976*	*1977*	*1978*	*1979*	*1980*[a]
Savings banks	19.2	21.6	18.0	13.0	11.7	11.0	9.8	9.7
Savings and loans	49.2	33.3	30.4	19.6	14.8	13.7	15.3	15.6
Credit unions	6.7	5.1	4.0	2.6	2.6	2.4	2.1	2.0
Commercial banks	4.0	5.7	5.9	5.3	6.0	5.9	5.9	5.7
Pension funds	5.1	7.1	7.7	10.0	11.4	11.5	9.8	9.5
Mortgage bankers	7.5	10.1	10.6	20.3	17.3	13.1	6.6	6.2
Nominees[b]	7.7	15.3	21.7	28.1	35.0	41.1	48.9	49.6
Individuals	0.5	1.9	1.6	1.1	1.2	1.4	1.6	1.7
Outstanding Volume	3.15	8.77	13.30	34.50	51.97	67.30	92.27	100.26

SOURCE: *Mortgage Banker* (July 1980).

a. Figures for 1980 are for May; all others are for December.

b. Largely pension funds, individuals, and trusts, but not specifically identifiable, owing to security registration rules.

Essentially, the development of mortgage-backed securities by GNMA and FHLMC has served two functions for the housing finance system. First, whole mortgages can now be represented by securities with characteristics that can be separately evaluated by the market, leading to a pricing process that is readily comparable to other securities regularly traded on financial markets. Thus, while an individual mortgage is of uncertain maturity and risk, the combination of the government guarantee and the risk-spreading effect of pooling converts the mortgage into an instrument (PTS) that may be compared to government bonds of like maturity.[9] This, in turn, has allowed the secondary market for mortgages to assume many of the characteristics of other bond and equity markets: GNMA securities trade on an active futures market and PTS options are themselves part of the large equities options market.

The second contribution of the development of federally sponsored mortgage-backed securities has been a demonstration effect. The positive experience of GNMA and FHLMC pass-throughs has proven the viability of this type of financial instrument. It seems likely that the market for private mortgage-backed securities will grow in the future, sustained by securities backed by conventional mortgages. By the end of 1980, however, this market had not yet appeared. Its development under Reagan's administration is addressed in chapter 5.

CHAPTER 5

HOUSING FINANCE UNDER REAGAN

The Reagan program in housing finance is aimed at several goals. The primary goal is the same as that of the administration's general economic program: to reduce the effect of the federal government on the economy, particularly on interest rates and prices. The mechanism by which this goal is to be achieved is the reduction of the size of federal expenditures, both direct and indirect, through credit and guarantee programs. In the latter area, the housing finance system presents an appealing target. Through GNMA guarantees of mortgage-backed securities, FHA mortgage insurance, FHLMC participation certificates, and the backup line of credit given FNMA, housing finance accounts for a major share of the contingent credit liabilities of the government. In addition, the mortgage lending industry, as structured through the seventies, allowed for further federal manipulation through deposit interest-rate controls, portfolio restrictions, and deposit insurance. Another major goal of Reagan's housing finance system, implied by a narrowing of federal control, is that of encouraging the private sector. Beyond these two general goals, the administration has sought also to foster the introduction of new mortgage instruments and to provide an adequate and affordable flow of funds to housing.

The desire to remove many, if not all, federal "intrusions" has shaped the budgetary and regulatory actions of the administration in housing finance. Although the regulatory actions were given momentum by the passage of DIDMCA in the last months of the Carter administration, the budgetary initiatives were instigated by Reagan. Because of the overlay of prior regulatory reform on Reagan initiatives, it becomes difficult to sort out cause and effect. Both the fiscal year (FY) 1983 and FY 1984 budget proposals include decreases in the authorization of funds for GNMA guarantees of mortgage-backed securities and FHA mortgage insurance. The Tandem mortgage-subsidy program operated by GNMA is to be phased out and deposit insurance allocations diminished.[1] In the regulatory area, the administration has promoted and secured passage of a program to complement and even go beyond the depository institution reform legislation of 1980. In addition, it has aggressively promoted the private mortgage-backed securities market by removing regulatory and tax barriers to the issuance of these instruments. However, the administration's intention to create a climate that will enable both FNMA and FHLMC to become fully private institutions is as yet unmatched by action.[2]

The record of success on administration initiatives in housing finance is, to date, scanty. The new proposals in the FY 1983 budget were rejected by Congress, with the result that the dollar reductions suggested for FY 1984 were scaled back. In general, there has been a great deal of debate within the administration itself as to whether the housing credit programs ought to be reduced at all, so the course of policy in this area remains an open issue.

The regulatory changes have proceeded somewhat more successfully, but have been prompted less by the actions of the administration than by the progress of the market. Private firms, particularly those relatively new to the mortgage market, have been developing investment instruments that meet (the quickly disappearing) federal regulatory requirements, yet are acceptable and desirable to market participants. FNMA and FHLMC have both been aggressive in developing new secondary market channels, but such initiatives imply a larger federal role in housing. It is thus possible that the administration's deregulatory actions will have been anticipated and discounted in the market by the time they are fully accomplished.

The rest of this chapter examines further the issues summarized above. The section immediately following discusses the nature of federal credit activities and the role of housing finance in them, as a backdrop to an analysis of Reagan's housing finance budget proposals. The third and fourth sections examine the regulatory and tax actions taken by the administration, and the final section describes events in the private sector and their present and anticipated effect on the housing finance system.

Budget Initiatives

Chapter 4 described the nature and growth of the federally related secondary-mortgage institutions. This growth has been partially responsible for an increasing federal presence in domestic credit markets. When GNMA issues a mortgage-backed security or FHA insures a home loan, a contingent liability is created that exposes the government to the possibility of full payment to the security holder or to the mortgagee. Similarly, because of the ties of FNMA and FHLMC to the federal government, borrowing by both of these corporations is construed by the market as federal borrowing. As these entities have grown, and as the government deficit has grown, the share of funds raised in domestic credit markets through the auspices of the federal government has increased from about 26 percent in 1977 to an estimated 54 percent in 1983.[3]

Given these patterns, it is understandable that the Reagan administration has attempted to curtail the growth of federal housing credit programs. Table 11 shows the composition of proposed changes in the total federal credit budget from actual FY 1983 levels to proposed FY 1984 levels (housing programs are indicated in the table note.) For direct loans, over 40 percent of the reductions would come from the Farmers Home Administration (FmHA) and from GNMA. For guaranteed loans, more than 150 percent of the *net* reduction would come from FHA activity. On top of this, the administration proposed for FY 1984 a $10 billion reduction in the guarantee authority under the GNMA mortgage-backed securities program. While, as indicated later in the chapter, these proposed changes were not approved by Congress, they represented a clear statement on the part of the administration as to its intent in the area of housing finance.

The proposals made for FY 1983, the first budget presented by the Reagan administration, provided an even clearer statement of the president's aims. This budget contained five initiatives:

1. Authorization for GNMA mortgage-backed securities was to be reduced by $20 billion.
2. Subsidized mortgage purchase activities (the Tandem programs) were to terminate in 1983, with residual funding declining to $1.1 billion by 1984.
3. FHA activities were to be targeted to individuals not currently served by the private market and the system made more efficient through the use of a single insurance fee charged at the outset of the loan.

TABLE 11

PROPOSED MAJOR CHANGES IN THE CREDIT BUDGET TOTALS, FISCAL YEAR 1983–FISCAL YEAR 1984

Budget Items	*Direct Loan Obligations ($ in Billions)*	*Guaranteed Loan Commitments ($ in Billions)*
Credit budget totals, 1983	49.1	102.7
Changes:		
International security assistance	—	0.3
CCC price supports and related programs	−3.8	−1.8
Farmers Home Administration[a]	−3.6	—
Education programs	—	0.6
Federal Housing Administration[a]	—	−6.1
Government National Mortgage Association[a]	−0.5	—
Veterans' housing programs[a]	—	1.2
Export-Import Bank	—	2.0
Small Business Administration	−0.2	—
Rural Electrification Administration	−0.5	−1.5
Other	−1.7	1.3
Total change	−10.2	−4.0
Credit budget totals, 1984	38.8	98.7
Memorandum: GNMA mortgage-backed securities *(secondary guarantees)*		−9.6

SOURCE: Office of Management and Budget, *Budget of the United States Government, Fiscal Year 1984,* Special Analysis (Washington, D.C.: GPO), p. F-8.

a. Federal housing programs.

4. FHA mortgage rates were to be deregulated and were to move with the market.[4]
5. Budget authorization for FmHA was to be reduced to $1.1 billion for new direct loans, a reduction of $2.6 billion from 1982 budget levels.

Each of these initiatives merits explanation here. The FY 1983 budget proposed that the maximum volume of mortgage-backed securities that GNMA could guarantee be scaled down from a level of $68.25 billion for FY 1982 to $48 billion in FY 1983. It was estimated that actual activity for both fiscal years would fall well short of these levels. Hence, these attempted reductions in GNMA's authority in both the FY 1983 and FY 1984 budgets represented in the short run a matter of principle rather than an effective attempt to cut the federal deficit. The initiative was based on the desire to remove a federal program that expands the contingent liability of the government and that competes directly with private entities. If GNMA could be scaled back, it was argued, the market would open up to private entrepreneurs. However, Congress did not concur.

The attempt to scale down GNMA in the FY 1983 budget failed, with Congress restoring previous authority levels. Congress did, however, approve the administration's request to phase out the Tandem assistance program. From a level of $2 billion in FY 1982, the program would end in 1983.

The administration's proposals for FHA's mortgage insurance programs were aimed at enhancing their low-income character, rather than directly decreasing the scope of the program. The objective here was to remove whatever competitive edge FHA had relative to private mortgage insurers and thus open the mortgage insurance industry to agencies outside the government. Accordingly, the FY 1983 budget request for FHA envisioned increases in loan applications and policies written through FY 1983 (by about 20 percent and 25 percent, respectively, above FY 1981 levels), but a decrease in FY 1983 commitment authority to $35 billion, from $40 billion in FY 1982. This would occur because insurance programs were increasingly directed toward lower-income households through an expansion of the graduated payment mortgage program and the institution of an insurance program for shared equity and variable rate mortgages. In addition, the U.S. Department of Housing and Urban Development (HUD) asked for an elimination of its power to set interest rates on insured loans, in favor of a system in which the rate was determined by the market.[5] Finally, the administration proposed a change in the insurance premium structure that would allow the payment of a single fee at the time of settlement, instead of a periodic mortgage payment addition.

While Congress did not reject explicitly the FHA proposals, neither did it adopt them. The result was that FHA expanded its graduated payment mortgage programs and has introduced a growing equity mortgage program (similar to a graduated-payment mortgage) but has gone no farther; it is still endeavoring to move to market-determined interest rates and a single insurance premium system.

In hindsight, it can be said that conditions in the economy in general and in the housing sector in particular caused the FY 1983 budget assumptions to be overly optimistic. Actual activity for both

FHA and GNMA mortgage-backed securities were both substantially overpredicted, so the lack of success by the administration in pushing its program in the federal credit area had no adverse (from its point of view) repercussions. In the FY 1984 budget, the attempt to cut back GNMA substantially was abandoned and proposed commitment levels scaled down only slightly from the 1982 level. In part this may be attributed to the unwillingness by Congress to accept lower limits, but it also stemmed from a desire on the part of the administration to keep open all possible avenues for a badly needed housing recovery. In the FY 1984 budget proposals, commitment levels for FY 1983 thus remain at $68.25 billion and are reduced to $58.65 billion for FY 1984. Again, these are substantially above the projected actual activity by GNMA in those years.

For FHA, the pattern is similar. The administration is once again trying to implement alternative mortgage programs, under the insurance function, and has included in the FY 1984 budget a demonstration of reverse annuity mortgages (a device designed to help elderly homeowners). Estimates of FHA activity have been increased significantly from FY 1983, in anticipation of continued low-interest rates and a strong housing recovery. Commitment authority is increased for 1983 in the FY 1984 budget, but the commitment declines in 1984 to actual 1982 levels. These figures are contained in table 12.

Regulatory Reform

During the first years of the Reagan administration, a number of housing finance reforms have been implemented that have carried on the momentum of the seventies but that also will have a crucial effect on the structure of the housing finance system of the future. Some of these reforms have been obvious successes and some have failed, but for a majority of the reforms, the verdict is still pending. The thrust of each reform has been the movement of the housing finance system into closer conjunction with other capital markets and the removal of governmental interventions from the system. While the system set up in the thirties was predicated on giving housing a sheltered financial channel, the new system would have all providers and users of funds bidding together in a private, lightly regulated market.

TABLE 12

REAGAN BUDGET PROPOSALS FOR FHA AND GNMA
($ in Millions)

Budget Items	*Actual 1981*	*Estimated 1982 (FY 1983 Budget)*	*Actual 1982*	*Estimated 1983 (FY 1983 Budget)*	*Estimated 1983 (FY 1984 Budget)*	*Estimated 1984 (FY 1984 Budget)*
FHA:						
Applications	550,296	610,000	410,558	660,000	907,000	817,000
Units insured	408,129	467,490	282,038	507,017	713,964	640,874
Amount of insurance	$16,069	$21,263	$11,193	$25,472	$37,528	$33,993
Commitment authority	$34,155	$40,000	$40,000	$35,000	$45,900	$39,800
GNMA:						
Commitment authority	$64,000	$48,000	$68,250	$38,400	$68,250	$58,650
Guarantees issued	16,853	28,500	13,515	32,000	35,240	39,100

SOURCES: U.S. Department of Housing and Urban Development, *FY 1983 Budget Summary* (Washington, D.C.: GPO, January 1982), pp. H-27, GNMA-7; U.S. Department of Housing and Urban Development, *FY 1984 Budget Summary* (Washington, D.C.: GPO, January 1983), pp. H-33, GNMA-7.

Many of the above-mentioned reforms were analyzed and recommended by the President's Commission on Housing. This body, constituted by President Reagan in June 1981, examined a wide range of issues related to federal and local housing policy. Its final report,[6] submitted in mid-1982, proposed a series of measures designed to reduce governmental presence in the housing sector.

The discussions following focus on the progress of reforms, addressed in the commission's report, that affect housing finance—specifically, deposit interest rates, assets powers and instruments, and business arrangements.

Liberalization of Deposit Rate Restrictions

As pointed out earlier in this book, DIDMCA had set up in 1980 a schedule for the elimination of deposit rate ceilings by 1986. In the wake of this legislation, a number of new savings instruments that carried relatively high interest rates as well as transactions accounts at all regulated institutions were introduced.

Within the framework of DIDMCA, the Depository Institutions Deregulation Committee designed, and the Congress passed into law in 1981, the All-Savers Certificate (ASC). This was a one-year savings instrument whose nominal interest rate was set at 70 percent of the current one-year Treasury-bill rate, but whose real return was enhanced by an exemption of this interest from taxation. Thus, an ASC that carried a 10 percent nominal rate would be the equivalent of a fully taxable instrument yielding 16.67 percent for the household in the 40 percent marginal tax bracket. The instrument was clearly designed to offer savers an alternative to short-term deposits, such as money market funds, at unregulated institutions. Moreover, since 75 percent of the funds raised through ASCs were to be earmarked for housing, the instruments would, presumably, bolster the housing sector.

Unfortunately, the ASC proved ineffective in both of its aims. First, the volume of funds placed in ASCs was lower than expected. Rather than the $40 billion–$70 billion predicted to be generated for savings and loans (the prime housing lender), ASCs had attracted only $20 billion by the end of 1981 (authorization date was October 31, 1981), and by the end of 1982 ASCs accounted for only one percent (about $7 billion) of savings and loan liabilities. Second, the ASC appears to have attracted little new money into regulated institutions; a majority of the deposits were transferred from other accounts at the same institution. Thus, the impact of the ASC was to increase the cost of funds to these institutions without increasing the resources available to them. Moreover, since the institutions involved are primarily housing lenders, the 75 percent set-aside had little marginal impact on the flow of funds to housing.

The reasons for the disappointing performance of the ASC are not immediately obvious. It is possible that the denomination requirement for the ASC dissuaded small savers from placing funds in the new instrument. A more probable explanation, however, is that the period of high interest rates and financial innovation that preceded the introduction of the ASC removed most of the interest-sensitive money from the housing finance system. Money market mutual funds won a place in the market by capturing the faith of the public, a public unconvinced that the rate advantage in the ASC merited moving funds out of the money market funds. The fact that so few funds were raised by the ASC relative to expectations and that most funds came from within the institutions themselves support the view that the public lacked confidence in the ASC.

The Garn–St. Germain bill sought to overcome this problem by authorizing a deposit account at regulated institutions that would be the equivalent of money market mutual funds and that would also carry the federal insurance that covered all other deposits. In mid-December 1982, these accounts were established with a minimum denomination of $2,500. The accounts have attracted some balances from outside the regulated institutions, but it is still too early to assess their long-term viability and impact. Their popularity is restricted by their minimum denomination, as was that of the ASC, but they are clearly competitive with the unregulated money market fund offerings.

One circumstance that argues for the near-term success of these new money market accounts is the state of the economy. Money market accounts were introduced at a time when short-term interest rates (and therefore the rate of return to money market mutual funds) were falling dramatically. The initial argument used to sell these accounts—that they were insured—proved sufficient to open up a market. It was easy to justify placing savings in uninsured vehicles when the rate of return was 13 percent, but less easy to do so when short-term rates were down to 8 percent and the economy was stagnating. Safety (i.e., insurance) assumed a greater priority in the portfolio of the average household.

Reinforcing this advantage is the transformation that has occurred in regulated institutions over the past several years. Pushed to the brink of extinction, savings and loan associations have begun to alter their operational mix and are becoming more attractive entities with which to do business. Financial reform has made it more worthwhile than before for a household to conduct its financial affairs through a thrift institution. The availability of a short-term investment account has certainly helped, but other services available as a result of the DIDMCA and the Garn–St. Germain bill also support the money market account.

A significant factor in the renaissance of regulated depository institutions has been the introduction (in 1981) of the universal Individual Retirement Account (IRA). This account carried a double tax sweetener: contributions were deductible from taxation and interest earned was not taxable. When the account was extinguished, the proceeds would be taxed as income, but the effect, nevertheless, is an interest-free loan from the government and permanent forgiveness of at least part of the tax liability on income. IRAs were a product of the deregulation at the end of the Carter administration, but were warmly endorsed and promoted by the Reagan administration because they increased the scope of private initiative in the financial area and decreased the burden of income taxation.

The IRA has proven a boon to the housing finance system. By September 1982, IRAs had drawn nearly $19 billion in mostly new resources to savings and loan associations. For the most part, these accounts are viewed as retirement savings vehicles. Thus, the funds that flow into thrift institutions and other housing lenders are likely to remain there for long time periods. This facilitates housing lending, since it allows the matching of assets and liability maturities.

The rapid growth of the IRA can be contrasted to the seeming failure of the ASC. The IRA offers long-term security for households in a form accessible to most. In terms of the housing finance system, however, timing and expectations are crucial. The IRA was not touted as the vehicle that would solve the housing recession. Rather, it was billed as a freedom-enhancing tax preference for retirement savings in a period when other forms of retirement income, notably Social Security, were becoming less certain. In fact, it has resulted in a rapid inflow of funds to savings and loan associations that, as a by-product, has provided significant funds for housing.

The final element in the deregulation of interest rates was the introduction, in January 1983, of high-interest transactions accounts. These "Super NOW" accounts carry variable interest rates but require high minimum balances. Together with IRAs, money market accounts, and the various savings accounts authorized as a direct result of DIDMCA, Super NOWs complete a set of debt-investment alternatives for the typical household.

The impact on regulated institutions has been an increase in the cost of funds. Since asset adjustments have taken place at a much slower pace than liability changes (asset maturities are much longer), the immediate effect has been a decline in profitability. For savings and loans in particular, this has pushed many over the brink of insolvency and has generated a shakeout of the industry.[7] Mergers, acquisitions, and failures have reduced the number of associations. However, those that remain tend to be full-service institutions and will prove quite profitable in the near term. This change is in keeping with the Reagan administration's philosophy of letting the market decide on the financial health of the firms in a given industry.

Assets Powers and Instruments

Although DIDMCA paved the way for the reorganization of liability portfolios, it accomplished remarkably little on the asset side. With the exception of the authority to place 20 percent of portfolio in consumer loans, commercial paper, and long-term corporate debt, DIDMCA did little to change the assets powers of thrift institutions. Other reforms concentrated on types of mortgages, but maintained the housing-finance focus of these institutions. The Garn–St. Germain bill, however, attacked the limitation of asset powers directly and gave thrifts power to invest in corporate and government securities with little or no geographic limitation. In addition, allowable portfolio shares for these investments will reach 20 percent by 1984. Thus, the two bills combined will allow thrifts to place up to 40 percent of their portfolios in nonmortgage assets. The implication of this legislation is increased stability for these institutions. In the past, thrifts have suffered from the struggle to support long-term fixed-rate assets with short-term, variable-rate deposits. With the liberalization of the assets and liability sides of the portfolios, assets-and-liability-matching (and thus a reduction of the risks inherent in financial intermediation) becomes a real possibility for thrifts.

The ability to achieve this result, however, will be limited by the tax situation that most thrift institutions face. Currently, thrifts receive a tax deduction tied to their mortgage lending if they maintain large percentages of their portfolios in mortgage-related assets. Thus, to be pursuaded to diversify their portfolios, institutions must be presented with an asset whose after-tax rate of return exceeds that of the tax-favored mortgage asset. Moreover, since the extent of the tax deduction decreases with the percentage of the portfolio devoted to mortgage assets, any shift not only directly affects the institution's rate of return but it indirectly changes the net return on all mortgages held. What occurs then is the shortening by thrifts of the asset portfolio's maturity through the purchase of mortgage-backed securities, which are more liquid than whole mortgage and yet qualify for the tax deduction.[8]

Potentially more important to the housing finance system has been the authorization of alternative mortgage instruments for federally regulated institutions. In 1975, state-chartered institutions in California were given the authority to acquire variable-rate mortgages under fairly stringent restrictions, and in 1977, FHA was authorized to offer graduated-payment mortgages. Thus, for several years these instruments have been in the public consciousness to some degree. In 1981, however, the FHLBB and the Office of the Comptroller of the Currency issued regulations that would allow their regulated institutions (savings and loan associations and national banks) to originate or acquire mortgages whose interest rates could be adjusted periodically. The power was similar to the increase in lending powers described above, in that it would allow these institutions to better match the maturities of their assets and liabilities.

In 1982, these new rules were liberalized to allow institutions to offer whatever terms they felt were justified by the market. In fact, the terms available on alternative mortgage instruments will become standardized as the secondary market describes the instruments it will purchase. As pointed out in chapter 4 and as discussed later in this chapter, the actions of the secondary market entities will be a major force in determining what occurs in the deregulated primary market. Because these rules are so new, however, and because secondary market institutions have not yet decided on the few types of alternative mortgages they will buy, little experience with the new instruments among mainstream firms has accumulated.

Eliminating Business Restrictions

Probably the greatest target of the Reagan administration in the housing finance area has been the body of laws and regulations that restrict the ability of firms and households to transact in mortgage markets. Geographic lending and branching restrictions, due-on-sale clauses, legal investment requirements, and chartering limitations have all acted to maintain the sheltered nature of the housing finance system and restrict the flow of credit to housing. These restrictions have all been attacked, through both the Garn–St. Germain bill and the individual actions of regulatory bodies.

The Garn–St. Germain bill eliminated geographic lending restrictions, limits on chartering, and the due-on-sale clause for all federally regulated financial institutions. These changes will allow thrift institutions and other mortgage lenders to service a variety of markets and export capital directly when profitable opportunities appear, rather than having to rely on the secondary market to perform this function. Thus, removing the barriers to the free movement of mortgage capital will decrease the cost of acquiring mortgage loans and increase the rate of return to the portfolios of these lenders.

The enforcement of the due-on-sale clause on all mortgage contracts except for FHA-insured or VA-guaranteed mortgages will enhance the ability of mortgage lenders to increase their portfolio returns as interest rates rise. Previously, the assumability of mortgages meant that when interest rates rose, low-rate mortgages would be passed on with the property as it changed hands. As a result, the lower-than-market-rate mortgages held by the lender would rarely pay off prior to maturity.[9] This is essentially what happened during the great real estate boom of the late seventies as seller financing, wraparound mortgages, and other creative financing techniques fueled the housing market. On the other hand, when interest rates fall, mortgages with high rates are paid off quickly and thus have a shorter-than-term life.

Enforcement of the due-on-sale clause furthermore takes away the assumability of mortgages and means that all properties will be refinanced at the market rate whenever they turn over. Both high- and low-rate mortgages will have shorter lives than the nominal term. In addition, lenders receive some protection, and their portfolios react more quickly to changes in market rate conditions. The preemption of state laws voiding due-on-sale clauses was a priority of the Reagan program and was supported by the housing finance industry.

The liberalization of chartering restrictions means that financial institutions that now operate under a mutual form of organization can convert to stock companies with relatively little problem. This will enable these firms to stabilize their long-term base by raising capital in the corporate market, beyond the capacity afforded by retained surplus. If a firm can increase its capital base, it can withstand the pressures and risks of financial intermediation, particularly in times of widely fluctuating interest rates. In addition, when interest rates fall, as they did in early 1983, conversion is especially attractive. Mortgage lenders with significant numbers of high-interest-rate mortgages in their portfolios become attractive buys and thus find it easy to raise capital as stock organizations.

Finally, individual agencies have moved to deregulate the investment restrictions that have kept institutions like pension funds out of the mortgage market. In early 1982, the U.S. Department of Labor included in its list of legal investments for public pension funds mortgage-backed securities of federally related agencies. While this is not complete removal of the limitation, it moves in the direction sought by the administration. This and other changes affecting the secondary mortgage market are discussed in the next section.

Secondary Market Changes

The policy of the Reagan administration to phase out GNMA has been accompanied by a policy to make FNMA and FHLMC fully private institutions. To date, the attempts have failed for two reasons. First, until the first quarter of 1983, FNMA had been experiencing severe losses. This reflects the maturity mismatch by which FNMA supports long-term mortgages with short-term debt. So long as its liabilities carry low interest rates due to the perceived federal connection, FNMA can viably carry low-rate mortgage. Without the federal backing, however, these low-rate loans would make FNMA financially vulnerable as a private firm. The second reason concerns FHLMC's recent attempt to become private. In early 1982, it proposed a major recapitalization that would have both severed some federal ties and granted it a status similar to FNMA. This effort failed and has made FHLMC somewhat reluctant to pursue further movement to private status.

Arguments for Privatization

The economic arguments for privatization of FNMA and FHLMC strike at both the regulatory and subsidy roles of the government's involvement. On the regulatory side, the argument can be made that regulatory constraints impede the institutions' adjustments to changing market opportunities and hazards, thereby bringing an unnecessary inefficiency to their operations.

The main argument against the subsidy to the secondary market institutions is that it causes a distortion in the allocation of capital in favor of the housing sector. Capital users in other sectors of the economy have to pay a higher relative price. The subsidy is real, even though there is no direct cash outlay by the government. The implicit federal guarantee of FNMA and FHLMC debt gives those institutions a distinct advantage in the capital markets, reducing their borrowing costs relative to private sector competitors. In the case of FNMA, that advantage currently is about fifty basis points compared to triple-A-rated corporate debt.

The second major form of subsidy is the exemption from SEC registration requirements applicable to private-sector debt issues. This exemption reduces the administrative costs of the federally sponsored agencies relative to those of competitors in the private sector.

The argument for privatization (i.e., withdrawal of the federal backstops) of FNMA and FHLMC is that while it may have been necessary for the government to demonstrate to the private sector that these activities were economically viable, continuation of the federal subsidy is now inhibiting the emergence of private-sector competition. The weaknesses of the primary market that FNMA and FHLMC were designed to offset—including credit rationing during tight money periods and the regional barriers to the flow of credit—have waned with the deregulation of the primary mortgage industry, and thus the need for the federally sponsored secondary institutions has waned also.

An added rationale for converting the federally related agencies to full private status concerns the manner in which FNMA operates. In effect, FNMA is a giant savings and loan association that finances long-term mortgages with short-term debt. The losses that FNMA suffered during the late seventies and early eighties were generated by the same adverse term-structure patterns that brought the thrift industry to a low point. In recent years, FNMA has labored to shorten its asset portfolio in order to reduce the risk of a recurrence of these losses. However, FNMA must still bear considerable interest-rate risk, which means that the federal government bears the risk, too. Unless a crucial social purpose is involved, there is little justification for this risk exposure.

No one has argued that the functions of the three secondary market institutions are no longer needed. They clearly are. The question, rather, is how much, if any, federal intervention in the operation of these institutions is appropriate.

Arguments against Privatization

Four arguments can be made against the privatization of the federally sponsored secondary market institutions.

The first is that housing cannot be treated merely as another commodity. Good-quality, affordable housing has been declared by Congress to be a national objective. Over the last fifty years the special status of housing has become codified in tax laws and other legislation favorable to the housing sector. If housing is a social good, then special subsidies to this sector of the economy may be justified.

A second argument against privatization is that some government control of the housing finance industry is required because the stakes are too high to allow the industry to collapse. The argument is the same as that applied against deregulation of commerical banking. The nation's past experience with bank failures and panics has made some observers wary of the risks of a freewheeling, unregulated, and highly concentrated financial sector.

The third argument is that fully private institutions could not be counted on to provide counter-cyclical support to the housing industry. In recent congressional hearings, the chairman of FNMA took understandable pride in pointing out that in 1982, the worst year for housing construction since the Second World War, FNMA purchased one out of every six home loans made.[10] Some argue that if the federally sponsored agencies were totally privatized, such aggressive action by private institutions to raise the troughs of the housing cycle would occur only as a profit-maximizing strategy.

Finally, it is argued that unregulated and unsubsidized secondary markets would not serve the housing needs of low-income households. Under current regulations, FNMA and FHLMC can purchase mortgages of up to $108,000 in value. This restriction provides modest targeting, as approximately 92 percent of all loans issued are below that amount. But FNMA and FHLMC have requested authority to purchase higher-valued loans, which would have the effect of eliminating even this modest targeting. GNMA's activities are aimed more at middle- and lower-income families because its securities are backed exclusively by FHA-VA mortgages, which are of lower average value than conventional mortgages.

Developments during 1980–1982

The Reagan administration has communicated its stance toward the secondary finance institutions in bits and pieces, rather than through a single statement. The policy must thus be divined by examination of budget requests, official testimony, and other public statements.

The picture that emerges is that the administration favors and is pursuing a gradual phaseout of the federal role. Privatization, especially the elimination of the government guarantee, is consistent with the general economic philosophy of the administration. The budget requests of the president have hammered away at the need to reduce government's role in the credit markets, and a phased reduction in GNMA's new commitments has been proposed each year.

> The Administration . . . remains committed to seeking the total privatization of two of the housing-related government-sponsored enterprises, the Federal National Mortgage Association and the Federal Home Loan Mortgage Corporation. Because of their Federal government sponsorship, these enterprises received special advantages in the securities market that completely private institutions do not have. An interagency Cabinet-level group will continue to pursue the goal of complete privatization of these enterprises.[11]

The Reagan administration has opposed legislation that would broaden the powers of FNMA and FHLMC without reducing their ties to the federal government. In 1982 the administration opposed a bill that would have permitted FHLMC to increase its capital base—which would have had the effect of increasing the amount of debt FHLMC could issue without increasing its interest rate. And in 1983 the administration opposed legislation that would have expanded the types and value limits of mortgages that FNMA is allowed to purchase.

The administration's actions to date have been directed more toward promoting new entry by private concerns into the industry than toward reducing the federal role in the current institutions. Foremost in this regard are the administration's efforts to eliminate unnecessary regulatory barriers to development of a private mortgage-backed securities program. In particular, regulations of ERISA, SEC, and the Internal Revenue Service (IRS) all put private securities at a disadvantage compared to government-sponsored mortgage securities. All of these regulations are now under close review, and some changes have already occurred.

As a group, these changes are intended to promote the use of Trusts for Investment in Mortgages (TIMs), thus producing an environment that enables private firms to craft a mortgage-backed security issue suited to a particular class of borrowers. As suggested in the pages following, the initial regulatory changes have already encouraged several private entities to enter seriously the secondary market. The last piece of the TIMs initiative, however, requires legislative action to adjust the tax status of these trusts. At present, such entities are subject to taxation at both the corporate and the personal level, which restricts their attractiveness. Removal of this barrier would open further the secondary market to private issuers, but has been slow in coming. As of mid-1983, achievement of the necessary tax changes was doubtful.

Here, again, doubts arise as to the consistency of administration policy and action. A current policy debate is whether the TIMs initiative should include FNMA and FHLMC. While, philosophically, the administration's answer ought to be in the negative, it has, to date, been unwilling to close the door completely.

The 1982 Report of the President's Commission on Housing laid out a blueprint for the phased withdrawal of the federal government from the secondary market.[12] While not officially embraced by the administration, the commission's recommendations offer a plan for achieving the goals the administration seemingly desires. The plan calls for removal of tax, legal, and regulatory impediments to widespread private investment in mortgages and mortgage-backed securities. These actions were spelled out in some detail by the commission, and the administration began moving on some of them, even before the commission submitted its final report. While offering far fewer specifics on the privatization of the current federally sponsored institutions, the commission expressed the opinion that "eventually . . . both FNMA and FHLMC should become entirely private corporations, without special access to the deep pockets of the Treasury or the Federal Home Loan Bank System."[13] As for GNMA, the commission argued for a "phasing down of the GNMA securities issues, timed to coincide with the reduction in FHA mortgage insurance, which would be restricted to those market segments that the private sector was unwilling or unable to serve."[14]

The President's Commission on Housing stopped short of calling for full privatization of FHLMC and FNMA. Rather, the commission envisioned the organizations as retaining an exemption from state and local taxes and as being required (through an undefined method) to continue to specialize in serving the secondary market for residential property loans. In this respect, the administration may well opt for a fuller privatization than that seen by the commission.

No legislation during the Reagan administration has significantly affected the secondary market—unlike the primary mortgage market, where continuing and accelerated implementation of DIDMCA and the Garn–St. Germain bill have had major impacts on savings and loan associations and their competitors. Despite the absence of legislation, FHLMC and FNMA have adjusted to the changing financial environment. Moreover, by broadening the types of mortgages they purchase (to include, for example, mobile homes, adjustable rate mortgages, and second mortgages), by diversifying their methods of financing those purchases, and by expanding the types of clients they serve, the two institutions have evolved into direct competitors. Previously FHLMC and FNMA issued different types of securities to different customers and bought mortgages from different institutions, with FNMA mainly serving mortgage bankers and FHLMC mainly serving savings and loans. Until recently, both institutions purchased only fixed-rate mortgages and did little to tailor their mortgage pools to the investment requirements of specialized customers such as pension funds. This situation has changed markedly in recent years.

GNMA has not been as innovative as FHLMC and FNMA and seems to be in a holding pattern while its fate is decided in the political arena. In fact, GNMA may have won a reprieve from further cuts, owing to its arguably key role in leading the way out of the 1980–1982 depression in the housing industry. As the industry began to recover in late 1982, FHA-insured mortgages accounted for approximately 25 percent of all mortgages written, a much larger share of the market than had been encountered in years immediately previous. Most of these mortgages were pooled by their originators and sold in the secondary market, carrying the GNMA guarantee. Without the guarantee, the securities could not have been sold at as low a yield, and therefore a higher interest rate would have been required on the mortgage, which would have deterred some home buyers.

Several noteworthy new institutions were established in the private sector in late 1982. The first is HOMAC (Home Mortgage Access Corporation), established as a subsidiary of the National Association of Home Builders. Designed to serve as an intermediary between the diverse, decentralized home builders and the secondary market, HOMAC pools loan requests from builders and in turn secures a FNMA commitment for those funds. The committed funds are then passed through a FNMA-approved lender, who originates and services the loan. The purpose of the program is to allow builders to tap directly the secondary market for mortgage funds. By providing financing to home buyers through this vehicle, HOMAC's ultimate intent is to stimulate new construction.

A second new institution is the Residential Funding Corporation (RFC). A subsidiary of Norwest Banc-Corporation, one of the nation's largest bank holding companies, RFC is designed to operate much like an unregulated FNMA or FHLMC. It will purchase residential mortgages—possibly $2 billion to $4 billion in 1983 alone—and finance those purchases with the sale of securities in the national market. The mortgages are insured by MGIC Corporation, the nation's largest private mortgage insurer, and the securities marketed through Salomon Brothers. The interest rate at which RFC is able to market its securities will give some indication of the financial market's assessment of the value of the federal guarantee. Unlike the federally sponsored institutions, RFC can and will buy large mortgages, above the $108,000 limit to which the federal institutions are currently restricted. Because of the subsidies afforded FNMA and FHLMC, it is primarily at this upper range that the private firms can expect to be competitive.

As nonfinancial institutions venture into the financial services industry, housing finance has been one target. The General Electric

Credit Corporation (GECC), for example, now has one-third of its financing activities ($3.5 billion) in housing. Since 1980, GECC has acquired mortgage banking and mortgage-insuring subsidiaries and has completed SEC registration of $300 million in mortgage-backed securities. More new entrants into the housing-finance industry can be anticipated as barriers are reduced and profitable opportunities arise.

Finally, new mutual funds for investment in mortgages are appearing. The first, the Mortgage Investors Fund, sponsored by the National Association of Realtors and the National Association of Home Builders, has the twin attractions of offering a market rate of return to its member-investors while at the same time channeling funds into their industry.

The Reagan Scorecard

As indicated at the beginning of this chapter, the efforts of the Reagan administration in the area of housing finance have been directed toward four goals: the reduction of the federal presence in the housing sector (both direct and indirect); the encouragement of the private sector; the expansion of the use of new mortgage instruments; and the assurance of adequate and affordable credit for housing. As with all sets of public policy goals, this one has inevitable internal conflicts. The provision of adequate and affordable housing can be fostered through the encouragement of the private sector over the long run, but the immediate reduction of the government's role means a reduction in housing affordability. Similarly, the introduction of new mortgage instruments may help lenders to cope with mortgage risk, but only at the cost of transferring this risk to borrowers, reducing once more the affordability of housing. Again, as with all sets of goals, priorities must be chosen; the administration's actions so far indicate which goals have been stressed.

The instruments and policy changes through which Reagan's goals have been pursued have been varied, ranging from the deregulation of the housing finance system to the desired conversion of federally sponsored, secondary market agencies into private firms. With an eye toward the long-term effects of these policies on the housing finance system, table 13 estimates their impact relative to the administration's program goals. Given the effects of all these policies, it is impossible to provide a summary evaluation of the

TABLE 13

GOALS AND POLICIES OF THE REAGAN HOUSING FINANCE PROGRAM

	Goals			
	Promote Capital Market Efficiency		*Stabilize the Housing Finance System*	
Policy Actions	*Remove Federal Presence*	*Encourage Private Market*	*Expand Use of New Instruments*	*Provide Adequate and Affordable Credit*
Authorize new instruments	o	+	+	?
Sunset on mortgage revenue bonds	?	–	?	–
TIMs	o	+	?	+
Privatize FNMA and FHLMC	+	–	o	o
Place constraints on GNMA	+	+	o	?
Limit FHA insurance	+	+	o	–
Financial deregulation	+	+	?	?

+ = positive with respect to goal.
– = negative with respect to goal.
o = neutral.
? = effect uncertain.

success either of individual policies or individual goals. However, some key points should be noted:

- For the most part, administration actions in housing finance have been neutral with respect to the flow of funds to housing. Given the rapid pace of events over the past few years, there is great uncertainty regarding the sources of future housing credit. Of actions either taken or continued by the Reagan administration in the area of housing finance, several will increase the adequacy and affordability of funds, several will decrease this adequacy and affordability, and others will have uncertain impact.
- Clearly, the administration would like to remove the federal presence in the housing finance system and encourage the private sector. The most important administrative action in this regard is the encouragement of the deregulation that had gained momentum during the late seventies. (However, this encouragement is less the result of administration initiative than of legislative momentum.) The proposed reduction in the capacity of GNMA to guarantee securities and of FHA to insure mortgages, together with the proposed movement of FNMA and FHLMC to full private status, also are geared to achieving these goals.
- With respect to new instruments, the administration has been essentially passive. The private sector has experimented with alternatives and taken the risks of implementation. The only major federal efforts in this area have been the FHA graduated-payment mortgage, and the adjustable-rate mortgage (ARM) regulations from the FHLBB and the Office of the Controller of the Currency.

On balance, the combination of deregulatory momentum generated before 1981 and steps taken by the Reagan administration in housing finance have set the stage for a more private, market-oriented system than in the past. The new system appears healthier than the old, and more flexible in periods of high and uncertain inflation. Indeed, flexibility in times of inflation is the crucial element in this whole process. As discussed in chapter 1, the course of housing finance is determined only partially by structural factors; the actual outcomes generated by the system depend to a large extent on the course of interest rates and prices. Future prospects in this regard are dealt with in the next chapter.

CHAPTER 6

THE FUTURE OF THE HOUSING FINANCE SYSTEM

The past decade has witnessed a profound change in the manner by which funds are directed into the housing sector. Basically, four factors have combined to transform relationships in the housing finance system. First, high and uncertain interest rates have altered the perceptions of the consumers of financial services as well as their behavior toward traditional depository institutions. As market rates exceeded regulatory ceilings, households placed lower values on conveniently located branch offices, automatic tellers, and free checking accounts. Funds flowed out of depository institutions and could be retained only at market rates. This in turn led to the second significant factor, the increasing share of short-term, market-rate liabilities in the portfolios of mortgage lenders. As of the end of 1982, about 63 percent of all savings and loan deposits were of less than one-year maturity, and a majority of the remainder were scheduled to mature in less than three years. Although declining interest rates and the new money market accounts have generated a strong flow of funds to these intermediaries, the pool of funds is too volatile to be used confidently for mortgage financing. Essentially, because of the short-term nature of their liabilities, thrifts must absorb greater risk in order to remain involved in housing finance.

Compounding this supply problem is a cost problem. Over the past decade, short-term rates have risen in both absolute and relative terms. More important, however, is that the degree of fluctuation of short-term interest rates has increased as well. Table 14 shows the pattern of rates for three-month certificates of deposit since late 1976. Up to the last two months of 1978, the series is relatively smooth, indicating that even if a mortgage lender financed

TABLE 14

THREE-MONTH CERTIFICATE OF DEPOSIT RATES, SECONDARY MARKET, LATE 1976–EARLY 1983

	Year							
Month	*1976*	*1977*	*1978*	*1979*	*1980*	*1981*	*1982*	*1983*
January		4.82	6.71	10.51	13.39	19.19	13.51	8.36
February		4.65	6.89	10.18	14.30	16.14	15.00	8.54
March		4.83	6.85	10.13	17.57	14.43	14.21	8.69
April		4.81	7.04	10.05	16.14	15.08	14.44	
May		5.20	7.42	10.15	9.79	18.27	13.80	
June		5.42	7.82	9.95	8.49	16.90	14.46	
July		5.46	9.00	10.11	8.65	17.76	13.44	
August		5.91	8.05	10.71	9.91	17.96	10.61	
September	5.26	6.18	8.61	11.89	11.29	16.84	11.66	
October	5.32	6.24	9.14	13.66	12.94	15.39	9.51	
November	5.13	6.68	10.72	13.90	15.68	12.48	8.95	
December	5.00	6.72	10.72	13.43	18.65	12.49	8.66	
Change from three months previous:								
January		−.50	.47	1.37	−.27	−4.25	−1.98	−1.15
February		−.48	.21	−.54	.40	.46	2.52	−0.41
March		−.17	.13	−.59	4.14	−4.22	1.72	0.03
April		−.01	.33	−.46	2.75	−4.11	.93	
May		.55	.53	−.03	−4.51	2.13	−1.20	
June		.59	.97	−.18	−9.08	2.47	.25	
July		.65	1.96	.06	−7.49	2.68	−1.00	
August		.71	.63	.56	.12	−.31	−3.19	
September		.76	.79	1.94	2.80	−.06	−2.80	
October		.78	.14	3.55	4.29	−2.37	−3.93	
November		.76	2.67	3.19	5.77	−5.48	−1.71	
December	−.20	.54	2.11	1.54	7.36	−4.35	−3.00	

SOURCES: U.S. Federal Reserve System, *Federal Reserve Bulletin,* various issues.

its assets through these short-term instruments, costs were fairly constant and predictable. Since November 1978, however, rates have fluctuated widely.[1] Coincidentally, these fluctuations have accompanied the increasing reliance of thrifts on shorter-term liabilities, causing large swings in the cost of financing mortgage investment.

Finally, the relationships within the housing finance system have been altered by a regulatory system that has struggled to keep abreast of the market. The increased risk absorbed by depository institutions has provoked deregulation, typified in DIDMCA and Garn–St. Germain, but the lag in regulatory action has heightened the sense of uncertainty on the part of mortgage lenders by pushing the housing finance system into a transition period.

The seventies began with the report of the Hunt Commission, which produced little direct action but nonetheless established an atmosphere conducive to change.[2] The commission's report consisted for the most part of the ideas that had been presented nearly a decade before by the Commission on Money and Credit. However, by 1970, the impact of inflation on the housing finance system was sufficiently apparent that the Hunt Commission's recommendations became a focus of reform efforts.[3] However, reform was to proceed through a political dialectic that generated fragmentary and often opposing actions.

For the most part, in fact, changes in the housing finance system have occurred in piecemeal fashion rather than according to a consistent plan. At times, these changes have strengthened the housing finance system against the unpredictable pattern of interest rates and inflation, while weakening other sectors of the economy. A prime example of this has been the efforts by thrift regulators to set a more liberal pattern for mortgage lenders. These efforts have occurred against the backdrop of an attempt by the Federal Reserve to restrain economic activity by restricting the flow of credit to housing. Evaluated from the restricted view of the housing finance system, the actions of the regulators have been beneficial; judged from the larger viewpoint of stabilization policy, the changes may not be so advantageous.

The future of the housing finance system will depend upon the consistency of regulatory reforms, both internally and relative to other aspects of public policy. Over the next several years, the actions of regulators together with the reaction of regulated institutions will shape the role of the housing finance system in supporting the housing sector and its relationship to the general course of economic activity. This chapter outlines the types of developments that will shape the future of the housing system and describes the expected role of the Reagan administration in affecting those developments. Briefly, the general areas that we judge most important to the future of the system relate to the sources of funds for mortgages, the portfolio behavior of savings and loan associations, development of the secondary mortgage market, and the relationships among institutions affecting the mortgage market and the macroeconomy. The sections following discuss the issues in each of these areas.

Mortgage Instruments and the Sources of Funds

Both the sources of mortgage credit and the instruments through which the credit is extended have changed in response to general financial reform. The variable interest rates of the seventies have caused lenders (and to some extent, borrowers) to become dissatisfied with the standard mortgage instrument. While the standard mortgage instrument remains the dominant vehicle for mortgage lending in the eighties, it exists as the most common of a number of different types of available contracts.

But what are the prospects for continued changes in the sources of mortgage credit and continued innovation in new mortgage instruments? The answer depends directly on the course of inflation. Should variable inflation with its attendant uncertainty become a permanent feature of the economy, mortgage lenders will use the new powers granted by the Garn–St. Germain bill to shorten the maturity of their assets, both to index them to the rate of price change and to match them more closely with their liabilities. This will tend to reduce the participation by these lenders in the mortgage market. Those who remain will make their adjustments by altering the manner in which they invest in mortgages.

The mortgage-backed securities developed by GNMA and FHLMC have proven to be popular vehicles for mortgage investment during an inflationary period. This popularity stems at least in part from the ability of mortgage lenders to use these instruments to reduce the average maturity of their portfolios, to recycle funds at market rates, and to tie themselves closely to the market. The fact the GNMAs are now regularly traded on futures and options markets makes them even more flexible vehicles for asset portfolio adjustment. Moreover, the GNMA experience has served as an example for the private sector. By absorbing the entrepreneurial costs associated with these securities, GNMA has afforded individual commercial banks and savings and loans the opportunity to issue their own securities under favorable conditions. Of course, if the Reagan administration limits both GNMA and FHA activity, other forms of mortgage-backed securities must be found. The major expansion of the market for mortgage-backed securities will then come from FNMA, FHLMC, and the private sector.

The sharp reduction in inflation over the last two years suggests that the inflationary expectations of the late seventies may in fact not be the norm of the eighties. Yet, the potential for the recurrence of rapid and variable inflation will mold the behavior of mortgage lenders. It seems unlikely that savings and loans as structured in the past will reappear. To the extent that savings and loans remain mortgage lenders, they will take on more of the character of a broker than an investor; loans will be originated for sale rather than for retention. To encourage this, FNMA and FHLMC have developed new purchase programs for different types of loans, so that traditional mortgage lenders will still serve the entire market.

Persistently high and variable inflation will also push lenders toward the use of alternative mortgage instruments. In addition, borrowers, especially first-time homebuyers, will be more attracted toward instruments that reduce the investment hurdle. The preference of lenders will push borrowers toward greater use of the newly authorized ARMs, since these closely track market interest rates. But while borrowers will opt for graduated-payment-type mortgages, they will tend to shy away from ARMs that do not offer attractive discounts.

Regardless of the dominant instrument of the future, a menu of mortgage instruments now exists sufficient to satisfy the needs of households in a number of life-cycle positions and economic circumstances. The GPM will be the province of the younger household with good income growth prospects; the sharing of home equity through a shared appreciation mortgage may appeal to high-wealth, low-income households who prefer to trade off future gain for current income; and elderly households may opt for a modified sharing of home equity, in which they sell off portions of their accumulated housing wealth for a guaranteed income flow. The issue for the future of the mortgage market is not what kinds of instruments will be present but the degree to which alternatives to the standard instrument will be used. If one assumes inflationary experience similar to that of the seventies, the eighties will see the end of the standard mortgage instrument as the dominant mortgage vehicle. If, on the other hand, inflation subsides *or* exhibits less variability, the standard mortgage instrument will remain the norm in mortgage markets, and alternatives will be available to those households whose circumstances warrant their use.[4]

The Portfolio Behavior of Savings and Loans

During the seventies, the balance sheets of savings and loan associations were significantly altered. On the liability side the passbook account, long the basic product line for associations, fell steadily and will continue to do so.[5] Concurrent with the decline in passbook accounts has been the increased attractiveness of intermediate-term, market-indexed certificate accounts. Various market-rate instruments of different maturities and denominations were introduced in the wake of DIDMCA and Garn–St. Germain and grew substantially. These liabilities can be expected to comprise the basic offering at savings and loan associations.

These deposit market trends are of concern because the flow of funds through savings and loan associations is important to the continued soundness of the housing finance system. Currently, savings and loan associations hold about 45 percent of all residential mortgages in the United States. Until such time as the mortgage market is more fully integrated into other capital markets, the ability of savings and loan associations to attract deposits will, to a great extent, determine the pool of funds available for mortgage lending. The future course of the housing finance system will be shaped significantly by the manner in which savings and loan associations adapt to the competitive pressures of the eighties. Three broad scenarios appear possible, described as follows:[6]

1. Associations will remain as they are, with portfolios of mortgage loans financed by variable-rate deposits. In this case, under the assumption that interest rates remain high, the majority of associations will go out of business or exist only as wards of the regulators; this is a highly unlikely scenario.
2. Associations will continue to support mortgage-lending activity but will react to the unavailability of low-cost liabilities by becoming mortgage brokers. This would entail originating mortgages to package in mortgage-backed securities, retaining the fees attached to the origination and servicing of the mortgages. Under these circumstances, the integration of the mortgage market into other capital markets would be hastened; this is a likely result for the larger savings and loan associations.
3. Associations will use their new powers to offer a complete set of services to households. In becoming "family financial centers," associations would provide transactions, trust, and savings services to households; offer first- and second-mortgage financing; and provide consumer installment lending through credit cards and direct loans. This development has

been envisioned by many associations for years and would be the likely choice of medium and small associations.

Although the course that will be taken by the savings and loan industry as a whole is unclear, it is fairly certain that associations will be unable to remain as they have been. Associations have a long way to go in learning how to use the asset and liability instruments newly available to them.[7] Assuming that the Reagan administration's initiatives continue, these freedoms will be increased. Thus, while the future cannot be predicted with any great accuracy, the coming decade will surely see a massive reeducation of savings and loan managers in how to operate in the new housing finance system.[8]

The Secondary Market

If the administration continues with conversion of FNMA, GNMA, and FHLMC to private status, a number of operational issues will have to be addressed. The phase-in has to be carefully orchestrated to retain the financial market's confidence in the institutions while simultaneously preventing any of the three from obtaining a competitive advantage over the others.

Privatization of FHLMC will probably be the most difficult. So long as its ownership remains exclusively within the savings and loan industry, the implicit federal guarantee will be hard to remove. FHLMC would not default on an obligation unless its owners—the nation's savings and loans—allowed it. Moreover, these owners would do anything in their power to prevent this default from occurring, as FHLMC exists as a service organization to them. If the savings and loans were unable to make good on the securities, the federal government would almost certainly intervene to prop up the associations, since the nation could not afford a loss of confidence in one of its main financial sectors.

However, if FHLMC were made a public corporation with its stock available for purchase in the open market, the linkage between the health of FHLMC and the health of the housing finance industry would be weakened, and the inevitability of federal intervention in the case of trouble would be removed, especially if the entry of new institutions into the industry had meanwhile reduced the relative importance of FHLMC to the industry at large.

The public selling of FHLMC would be the single most important step toward privatization, but it would be the last step in a long process. A series of changes would have to precede this, so that investors would have a good sense of what they were buying.

These changes, which could occur simultaneously, are as follows:

- Elimination of exemption from income tax
- Elimination of the ceiling on capitalization
- Elimination of the SEC waiver
- Elimination of restrictions on the type and amount of mortgages held and other congressional and HUD oversight restriction

FNMA is farther along the course to privatization than FHLMC. FNMA already is a publicly traded stock, the corporation pays income tax, and it has no explicit limits on its capital base—it can issue additional stock with the consent of HUD. However, the federal government continues its oversight role and FNMA's activities are subject to HUD approval.

But FNMA, unlike FHLMC, has a backstop line of credit with the Treasury. Until the first quarter of 1983, FNMA had been operating in the red for several years, caught like many savings and loans in the squeeze between low-yield, long-term assets and high-interest, short-term liabilities. Without the Treasury backstop, FNMA would have had a more difficult time weathering the past years' difficulties. Privatization of FNMA would be predicated on removal of the backstop line of credit at the Treasury, combined with elimination of the restrictions on FNMA activities and elimination of the SEC exemption. This process will need to proceed slowly and delicately to avoid a severe disruption in the housing finance system.

Finally, the credibility of the federal disengagement from FHLMC and FNMA depends vitally on the emergence of new actors in the marketplace. As long as FNMA and FHLMC together continue to account for the majority of all secondary market activity, the financial markets will probably correctly perceive that the federal government could not allow these institutions to fail.

FHLMC and FNMA have become direct competitors in the markets for both assets (mortgage) and liabilities (securities). In recent congressional hearings, FNMA came out strongly against FHLMC's request for the power to expand beyond its current capital limits.[9] FNMA argued that FHLMC already has a competitive advantage of income tax exemption over FNMA and that any new freedoms for FHLMC should be coupled with its conversion to taxpayer status. With the two organizations offering more or less the same products to the same market, it will be increasingly important that they compete on an equal footing. One might contend that it makes no sense for two government-sponsored institutions to duplicate each other's functions; nonetheless, market competition would be promoted by having both survive as competitors in a fully private arena.

GNMA's movement to the private sector can proceed on a somewhat different track from FHLMC and FNMA. The President's Commission on Housing discussed two possible ways of doing this. One is a preannounced, gradual phaseout of the GNMA securities program. The second, and more efficient, approach is a gradual increase in the fee GNMA charges for its guarantee, until the fee reaches a level that will yield a profitable return to private-sector institutions, thus precipitating their entry.[10] The question then becomes that of determining GNMA's proper role as one of several actors in that market. Realistically, GNMA could either wind down its level of business (presumably approaching or reaching zero) or specialize in supporting the lowest end of the market, say, the bottom 20 percent of the mortgage value distribution. Complete transfer of GNMA to the private sector is unlikely, since it is not clear what the private sector values aside from the federal guarantee.

The freedom of activity implied by privatization raises the question of whether FHLMC and FNMA would venture into new business areas, becoming perhaps "financial supermarkets" of the sort now evolving in the financial services industry. Some diversification seems probable, but FHLMC and FNMA will almost certainly continue to specialize in the business they know best, especially since the secondary mortgage market will probably expand for the foreseeable future.

To reiterate, the success of any privatization of the secondary mortgage market depends on the emergence of new players in the private sector. As long as federally sponsored institutions are the dominant actors, the implicit federal guarantee will remain. Any failure to make good that guarantee, if ever required, would have calamitous consequences for the housing finance industry and for a substantial proportion of all Americans.

The transition problems described above are not trivial. But let us assume that they are overcome. What are the ultimate consequences for American consumers once the new, fully private housing finance industry is in place and functioning?

Past studies provide useful evidence of the effects of the current institutions on housing finance. These studies allow one to forecast the effect of privatizing the federal institutions, since this effect should be less than that of total elimination of the institutions. While evidence is limited and not entirely consistent, it appears that FNMA's and FHLMC's activities in the secondary market have substantially influenced interest rates—perhaps as much as a percentage point during the period 1965–1975. On the other hand, there has been little net effect on the amount of credit provided, as the purchases of mortgages by the federal institutions have reduced the profitability of this function for private sector actors—mainly insurance companies—who have as a result withdrawn from the market.[11]

Despite the modest long-term effects of FHLMC and FNMA on the amount of mortgage credit, the evidence is that the institutions have had a significant impact on smoothing the housing cycle, providing liquidity to primary lenders during periods of tight credit, and being relatively less expansive during periods of loose credit.[12] Thus, one of the major objectives of these institutions, as envisioned in their formation, has in fact been achieved.

The housing finance environment has changed considerably since the sixties and early seventies, the time periods covered by the studies just described. The housing finance cycle has been dampened due to deregulation of the primary market, which has resulted in continuous availability of housing credit, albeit at a price that reflects credit market conditions in general. The absolute and relative size of the secondary market has expanded considerably, owing to near-explosive growth in demand for mortgage credit combined with only modest growth in the traditional source of mortgage credit supply—deposits in thrift institutions. This expansion may mean that the impact of the federally sponsored agencies on the housing sector and credit markets in general is now greater than it was previously. It seems most probable that successful privatization of FNMA and FHLMC would result in a modest increase in the cost of mortgage credit, adding less than one percentage point to the rate charged on the typical mortgage, arising from the loss of the federal guarantee.[13]

What about GNMA? Any scenario for privatization would involve an increase in the cost of credit to the home buyers now served indirectly by GNMA. The GNMA fee for its guarantee is set currently at six basis points. Opinions vary as to the fee that a private organization would have to charge to provide a comparable guarantee.[14] However, although the fee will be higher than the current GNMA fee, it is unlikely to be more than 100 basis points. The distributional impact of GNMA privatization would be greater than that of FNMA and FHLMC. This is because GNMA serves the middle and lower end of the income distribution, guaranteeing only pools of VA and FHA mortgages, which currently can be for no more than $90,000.

As stated, the distributional impact of FHLMC and FNMA privatization will be less and will benefit higher-income homebuyers. Currently, the two institutions can purchase loans up to only $108,500 in value. If the institutions go private, this restriction will be lifted. The primary lenders would have an additional outlet for large mortgages, and this may reduce slightly the rate of interest at which they are willing to make these loans to higher-income homebuyers.

The successful privatization of the secondary mortgage market will probably have only a modest negative effect on the quantity of mortgage credit provided in the marketplace. The effect on home-mortgage interest rates will be relatively greater, but will still raise mortgage rates by less than a percentage point. Higher-income households may have their mortgage rates reduced slightly through privatization, whereas a small increase in rates for lower-income borrowers seems certain.

If everything goes smoothly, the overall effects of privatization should be modest. The real danger comes if the transition does not proceed smoothly. For example, if the financial markets should lose confidence in one of the newly privatized institutions while these institutions were still dominant in the market, this could have a severe effect on the housing industry. Nor could the newly privatized institutions be expected to provide countercyclical support as they have in the past, unless such support coincided with their profit-maximizing objective. If GNMA remained in existence as a government organization, it could be called upon as needed to provide countercyclical support and other special assistance on an ad hoc basis.

If the net effects of full privatization of the federally sponsored housing-credit institutions are modest, then one must ask whether the likely gain is sufficient to offset the risk of the transition. The Reagan administration has decided that it is worth it. The next two years will tell whether the administration is willing to move forcefully to bring about the transition.

Relationship between Housing Lenders and Macroeconomic Policy

Finally, we need to speculate on the nature of the institutions that will serve the housing finance system in the future and the implications of the form of those institutions for the conduct of macroeconomic policy. Regardless of whether the eighties are characterized by the high and variable inflation rates of the seventies or whether the administration's antiinflation policy works in the long run, we predict that the degree of specialization that has existed among housing finance institutions will diminish. Because of the opportunities available in the secondary market and the deregulation efforts of the Reagan administration, it appears likely that most institutions, particularly commercial banks and life insurance companies, will initiate mortgage-backed securities as regular parts of their portfolios and will be joined by new, private entities. Conversely, savings and loan associations will move further away from the mortgage investment business and will adapt to the new powers afforded them to diversify their portfolios.

These changes, however, will present three types of challenges to the government's typical manner of dealing with the housing finance system. First, a given monetary policy objective requires a larger change in the money supply. Up until the seventies, monetary policy could reasonably be expected to operate primarily through the housing finance system. Since mortgage markets were segmented and mortgage rates generally more sluggish than other interest rates, restrictive monetary policy would draw funds out of the mortgage market and thus slow down housing construction. The resultant unemployment would ripple through the economy and lead to a general economic slowdown. The integration of the mortgage market with other financial markets, however, will mean that funds will no longer be readily drawn from the housing finance system. Under such a system, mortgage and deposit rates will adjust as necessary to maintain the flow of funds into housing, and the burden of monetary policy will fall elsewhere.

These events entail a slower transmission process for monetary policy. The corollary to this is that a restrictive monetary policy will bite longer and harder on the economy as a whole than in the past. The prolonged recession of 1981 and 1982 is typical of what will happen in the future should inflation again leap up. Either the

Federal Reserve must resign itself to employing monetary actions of greater magnitude than in the past in order to implement policy, or the policy process needs to be reconsidered.

Second, the general integration of mortgage markets into the broader capital market will alter the structure of interest rates. Without the artificial constraints of a regulated market, mortgage and deposit rates will be free to adjust quickly and fully to changes in market conditions and inflation expectation.[15] Not all institutions, however, will be able to compete in an unregulated environment, and some will face solvency problems to a degree previously not experienced. In this situation, the structure of the financial services industry will change. In order to secure a more reliable capital base, many mutual institutions will use their new powers and convert to stock companies, raising funds on equity markets. In addition, merger activity will increase as stronger institutions absorb weaker ones. The result will be fewer and larger institutions of all kinds.[16]

Increased mortgage interest rates will also mean greater cash-flow constraints for borrowers. While the cost of homeownership will still be reduced by the tax preferences connected to owner-occupancy, the income and capital constraints faced by prospective homebuyers will continue to be a housing market problem. As discussed earlier, the exapnded use of alternative mortgage instruments will mitigate this problem to a certain extent, and the persistence of inflation will increase the use of these instruments.

The changes that have occurred in the financial environment imply that the role of the regulator must change as well. This is particularly true in the case of the Federal Home Loan Bank system. Since savings and loan associations now have a variety of sources of funds under DIDMCA, Garn–St. Germain, and other regulatory changes, the supervisory functions of the Federal Home Loan Banks will necessarily intensify. Associations, unused to dealing in the new markets to which they have access, will almost inevitably make miscalculations that will endanger their financial viability. The FHLBB, with both its supervisory and insurance functions, has the ability and responsibility to see that such problems are avoided in the future, especially as associations begin to use their increased borrowing possibilities. The role of FHLBB advances as a defensive tool also becomes more important as associations proceed with the refunding of outside borrowing.

Finally, coordination among regulatory agencies must increase. Currently, the Federal Home Loan Bank Board, the Federal Deposit Insurance Corporation, and the Office of Comptroller of the Currency govern various overlapping areas of financial regulation. In part, this is a reflection of the extensive regulation of the housing finance system. As the system becomes more connected to the free market, this layering will diminish. However, those agencies that do remain will need to work together if the new system is to flourish.

NOTES

Notes to Chapter 1

1. The Nixon wage- and price-freeze in 1971 was designed to remedy the "crisis" of 4 percent inflation, a rate the inflation-weary public would have been happy to see in 1983.

2. *Report of the President's Commission on Financial Structure and Regulation* (Washington, D.C.: U.S. Government Printing Office (GPO), 1972); U.S. Congress, House, Committee on Banking, Housing and Urban Affairs, *Financial Institutions and the National Economy: Discussion Principles*, 1975; U.S. Federal Reserve System, Board of Governors, *Ways to Moderate Fluctuations in Housing Credit* (Washington, D.C.: GPO, 1972).

3. Although these measures provided the means for thrift institutions to maintain their solvency and viability in an uncertain world, their effects were dampened by the tax incentives to hold mortgages that still apply to thrifts. Under Section 593 of the Internal Revenue Code, savings and loan associations that hold 82 percent of their assets in housing-related securities can deduct 40 percent of their gross income from their taxable base. This means that the net after-tax return on mortgages to thrifts is enhanced to the point that they dominate other assets. Thus, while the financial reform bills gave thrifts the power to diversify, the tax system gives them incentive to remain predominantly mortgage lenders.

4. *Report of the President's Commission on Housing* (Washington, D.C.: GPO, 1982).

Notes to Chapter 2

1. In this book, *housing finance system* refers to the arrangements and institutions that facilitate the financing of residential buildings. In practice, we will concentrate on the financing of the acquisition of one-to-four-family housing, since this subsector of the housing market has traditionally been the major focus of national housing policy.

2. FHA has served so well that it has spawned a thriving private mortgage-insurance industry that has bid away a significant portion of FHA business.

3. Prior to the entrance of FHA into the market, self-amortizing mortgages were much less common than now. Many mortgages were of the balloon type: although the interest rate was fixed, regular payments covered interest only, with the entire

principal due at maturity. If (as was the case in the depression) times were bad when the mortgage note came due, default was almost unavoidable. Self-amortizing mortgages provided that the principal be paid down regularly, thus avoiding the balloon payment problem.

4. The best description of the process that resulted in this mortgage market configuration can be found in Saul B. Klaman, *The Postwar Residential Mortgage Market* (Princeton, N.J.: Princeton University Press, 1961).

5. The domination of the housing market by FHA during the war years is a result of the generally low rate of private housing production. Note that up to the mid-1950s, FHA volume grew in numbers of units insured in each five-year period.

6. For more detail, see Klaman, *Postwar Residential Mortgage Market*, chapter II.

7. The figures in the text refer only to one-to-four-family units insured and are derived from Klaman, *Postwar Residential Mortgage Market*, table 4.

8. Insurance companies built origination and servicing capacity for multifamily residential and nonresidential real-estate lending and later shifted their portfolios in the direction of these loans.

9. The return of this spread to previous levels in the late seventies was accompanied by a modest return to the mortgage market by discretionary investors.

10. The financing of long-term, fixed-rate mortgage holdings through the issuance of short-term, variable-rate deposits is profitable so long as the institution can accurately forecast the pattern of short-term interest rates over the life of the mortgage. The life of the mortgage, in the absence of good secondary-market facilities, is dependent upon repayment patterns. In periods of rising rates, the average life of the mortgage rises as well, since prepayments fall. This introduces a problem for lenders. In the presence of an active secondary market, however, this problem is diminished, as lenders have more control of the time period over which they will hold the mortgage. In this case, mortgage rates could be set in such a manner that the lender generates a surplus over the portfolio planning horizon. Over the life of the mortgage, there will be negative cash flow when deposit rates are above the average rate on the mortgages held in the portfolio, and positive cash flows when the reverse occurs. The net flow over the entire life of the mortgage should be positive if the lender has accurately predicted deposit rates and set the mortgage rate so that it equals, in present value, the average short-term deposit rate over the holding period of the mortgage. (For a full analysis, see George G. Kaufman, "A Proposal for Eliminating Interest Rate Ceilings on Thrift Institutions," *Journal of Money, Credit, and Banking*.) Since the profitability of mortgage lending is positively related to the predictability of future interest rates, volatile interest rates reduce the attractiveness of mortgage lending. If lenders underestimate the future pattern of short-term interest rates, mortgage lending will generate losses that eventually drive lenders out of business. Yet, if lenders attempt to hedge by posting mortgage rates high enough to cover their worst-case guess for the future, mortgage demand falls, and lenders find themselves with unplanned excess liquidity.

11. The Home Owners Loan Act of 1934 established the thrift industry for the purpose of financing housing, and subsequent regulatory and insurance legislation is predicated on savings and loan mortgage investment. Also, tax laws allow savings and loans significant relief from taxation (they were given full exemption from federal taxes until 1962) if these institutions maintain the vast bulk of their assets in mortgage loans. It should be noted that about the time that tight monetary policy and inflation were wracking havoc with interest rates, the tax preference for savings and loans was being eliminated. This compounded the problems of savings and loans in their efforts to be viable mortgage lenders. A complete analysis of the tax question is found in Kenneth R. Biederman and John A. Tuccillo, *The Taxation and Regulation of the Savings and Loan Industry* (Lexington, Mass.: Lexington Books, 1976).

12. Robert A. Taggart, Jr., and Geoffrey Woglom, "Savings Banks' Reactions to Rate Ceiling and Rising Market Rates," *New England Economic Review* (Federal Reserve Bank of Boston), September/October, 1978), pp. 17–31.

13. On the demand side, increased mortgage rates as a consequence of monetary policy actions reduced the ability of households to buy homes.

14. Recessions are "officially" dated by the National Bureau of Economic Research (NBER). The most recent recession has been officially defined as beginning in June 1981.

15. The most recent cycle appears to be following this trend, as its recovery (still underway in August 1983) has exhibited the largest percentage change in housing starts in the postwar period.

16. The Hunt Commission's report, issued at the end of 1972, provided a blueprint for the effective deregulation of the housing finance system. It also spawned numerous other reform efforts. For a full discussion of these reform efforts, see U.S. Department of Housing and Urban Development, "Current Initiatives for the Reform of the Housing Finance System," by John A. Tuccillo and Kevin E. Villani, in *Occasional Papers in Housing and Community Affairs*, vol. 9 (Washington, D.C.: GPO, March 1981), pp. 261–293.

Notes to Chapter 3

1. Consumer Price Index numbers can be found in the *Economic Report of the President* (Washington, D.C.: GPO, 1979), p. 263; housing price inflation data are derived from U.S. Department of Commerce, Bureau of the Census, *Construction Reports*, series C-25, various issues. The figure in the text refers to that for an average-quality new house sold in 1974 and therefore corrects for size or other quality changes that might occur in the typical new house sold.

2. The impact of inflation on interest rates is conventionally described through the "Fisher effect," which hypothesizes that the rate of interest will rise point for point with the rate of inflation (see Eugene F. Fama, "Short Term Interest Rates as Predictors of Inflation," *American Economic Review*, vol. 65, no. 3 (June 1975), pp. 269–282. The problem with this hyothesis is that high rates of inflation are also quite variable, thus introducing a degree of uncertainty as to whether the interest rate has adjusted to fully reflect the course of inflation over the period of the contract. This uncertainty further decreases the attractiveness of assets whose return is fixed in money terms. Assets, like houses—whose return takes the form of a stream of services that rise in value as prices rise—or like corporate equities—whose return is (at least potentially) indexed to inflation—are preferable if inflation rates are high and/or variable.

3. An outgrowth of this disintermediation process was the development by the unregulated sector of the financial market of a number of new instruments to accommodate the switch by households out of regulated instruments. While regulated instruments were inferior in terms of return, they offered the convenience of investing small amounts for brief periods. Most households, particularly small savers, could not accommodate either the large denominations or the relatively long maturities in the bond market. This led to the increased popularity of mutual funds and the invention of a new form of mutual fund that held short-term assets and offered relatively low denomination shares. The growth of the money market mutual funds, especially during the late 1970s, was extremely rapid. From an asset base of about $4 billion in 1975, the funds grew to a volume of nearly $80 billion by the middle of 1980. For an analysis, see Timothy Q. Cook and James G. Duffield, "Money Market Mutual Funds: A Reaction to Government Regulations or a Lasting Financial Innovation?" *Review* (Federal Reserve Bank of Richmond), July/August 1979.

4. Patric H. Hendershott and Kevin E. Villani, *Regulation and Reform of the Housing Finance System* (Washington, D.C.: American Enterprise Institute, 1977), table 7.

5. The most significant of these new instruments was the money market certificate, a six-month security that carried an interest rate similar to the rate of U.S. Treasury Department bills.

6. Stephen T. Zabrenski, "Changes in S&L Account Structure: October 1979–March 1980," *Federal Home Loan Bank Board Journal*, vol. 13, no. 8 (August 1980), pp. 21–29; and Richard G. Marcis and Dale Riordan, "The Savings and Loan Industry in the Eighties," *Federal Home Loan Bank Board Journal*, vol. 13, no. 5 (May 1980), pp. 2–15.

7. Besides draining funds out of assets that carry a fixed, money-dominated return into assets that are indexed to the market, inflation also channels funds into residential investment, as opposed to other forms of capital assets. The cause of this bias toward housing is the fact that the tax system combines with inflation to produce extraordinary gains from investment in housing relative to other forms of investment. Those who invest in owner-occupied housing are allowed to deduct from income some of the expenses associated with homeownership—mortgage interest and property tax payments—and need not recognize as income the flow of services derived from ownership of the housing unit. On the other hand, the income generated by investment in plant and equipment is taxable, and some of the expenses of this investment—notably depreciation—are deductible but calculated at rates that do not reflect the course of inflation. The chief problems for a firm with respect to the tax treatment of investment are the use of historical costs to calculate depreciation deductions and the conventional use of FIFO inventory accounting systems. In periods of rapid price inflation, both these methods understate deductions and therefore overstate taxes. It has been estimated that inflation has raised the marginal tax rate on corporate income to well over 65 percent (see M. Feldstein and L. Summers, "Inflation and Taxation of Capital Income in the Corporate Sector," Working Paper 312 [New York City National Bureau of Economic Research, 1979]). The result of this bias is the gradual diversion of capital from plant and equipment investment toward residential investment. This shift is important in two respects. First, the increased residential investment is less productive in the long run than plant and equipment investment, since the former does not build the same productive capacity. A relative increase in residential investment will lower long-term growth rates. Second, in the short run, residential investment is less productive, since it is taking the form of appreciation of existing structures rather than that of new construction.

8. Because such a large sector of the mortgage market is subsidized, either directly or indirectly, mortgage rates tend to lag other market rates in fully adjusting to inflation. The direct subsidy is represented by programs like GNMA's Tandem program, which offered mortgages to qualified borrowers at interest rates below the market. When full accounting was made not only for the lack of full adjustment of mortgage rates to the rate of inflation but for the tax deductibility of mortgage-interest payments and the fact that service flows and capital gains from owner-occupied housing are not recognized as income, the cost of capital to the homeowner was significantly lower than the cost of other forms of capital. Recent analysis indicates that this cost may be as little as half the cost of plant and equipment investment—see Patric H. Hendershott and S.C. Hu, "Inflation, Taxes, the Mortgage Contract, and the Benefits from Owner-Occupied Housing," *Public Finance Quarterly*, vol. 10, no. 2 (April 1982), pp. 158–184. Because of these benefits, higher-bracket taxpayers will actually receive a capital *subsidy* at high rates of inflation. The exact cost of capital sustained by the homeowner will depend not only on tax bracket and inflation rate, but also the terms under which the house was purchased. Recently,

mortgage rates have adjusted more fully to inflation, and housing prices have risen at slower rates. Thus, recent home buyers are not reaping the extraordinary gains that have accrued to earlier buyers. However, in relative terms, housing still remains the one investment available to the average household that is yielding a positive, real, after-tax return. Added to these inducements to investment in owner-occupied housing is the long-term benefit of the fixed-rate mortgage. The standard mortgage instrument calls for a fixed series of payments over the life of the mortgage. In real terms, the value of these payments falls during periods of inflation. Theoretically, lenders will recognize this fact and increase mortgage rates to reflect it. This will "tilt" the pattern of mortgage payments by increasing their real value in early years over that prevailing in a zero-inflation world to compensate for lower real value later in the life of the mortgage. For an analysis of this process, see F. Modigliani and D. Lessard, *New Mortgage Designs for Stable Housing in an Inflationary Environment* (Federal Reserve Bank of Boston, 1975).

9. Patric H. Hendershott and S.T. Hsieh, "The Growth in the Volume of Mortgage Credit, 1968–78," paper presented at the meeting of the Southern Economic Association, Atlanta, 1979.

10. A recent paper by Edward J. Kane, "Consequences of Contemporary Ceilings on Mortgage and Deposit Interest Rates for Households in Different Economic Circumstances," in *The Government and Capital Formation*, ed. G. von Furstenberg (Lexington, Mass: Ballinger Publishing Co., 1980), based on a careful examination of the ownership of passbook accounts, indicates that for the typical account holder, the nominal after-tax return has averaged 3.68 percent since 1966. With the rate of inflation averaging 6.2 percent over the same period, the real return to passbook accounts averaged −2.52 percent.

11. Material in this section is drawn from U.S. Department of Housing and Urban Development, "Current Initiations for the Reform of the Housing Finance Systems," by John A. Tuccillo and Kevin E. Villani, in *Occasional Papers in Housing and Community Affairs*, vol. 9 (Washington, D.C.: GPO, March 1981), pp. 261–293.

12. For analyses of the effect of the experiment, see Timothy Q. Cook, "Regulation Q and the Behavior of Savings and Small Time Deposits at Commercial Banks and Thrift Institutions," *Review* (Federal Reserve Bank of Richmond, November/December 1978), pp. 8–15; and Edward J. Kane, "Getting Along Without Regulation Q: Testing the Standard View of Deposit Rate Competition During the 'Wild Card' Experience," *Journal of Finance*, vol. 33, no. 3 (June 1978), pp. 921–932.

13. The MMC rate at thrifts originally floated 0.5 percentage points above T-bill rates; the rate of banks would carry a premium of 0.25 points. In February 1979, continuous compounding of interest on MMCs was discontinued, and by midyear the thrift differential was eliminated. This removed some of the attractiveness of the MMC relative to a T-bill. In early 1980, the rate advantage of thrifts over commercial banks was removed, except in those cases where T-bill rates fell below 9 percent.

14. For a more in-depth explanation of this "tilt" in real payments and its impact on households, see Modigliani and Lessard, *New Mortgage Designs for Stable Housing*.

15. A great deal has been written about alternative mortgage instruments. The most comprehensive treatments are found in Modigliani and Lessard, *New Mortgage Designs for Stable Housing*; and Donald Kaplan, Richard Marcis, and Henry Cassidy, eds., *Alternative Mortgage Instruments Research Study* (Washington, D.C.: Federal Home Loan Bank Board, 1977). In addition, specific aspects of these instruments are discussed in Raymond J. Struyk and James Follain, "Homeownership Effects of Alternative Mortgage Instruments," *AREUEA Journal*, vol. 5, no. 1 (Spring 1977), pp. 1–75; Robert M. Buckley and John A. Tuccillo, "An Analysis of Non-Level Payment Mortgages," in *Capital Markets and the Housing Sector*, ed. Robert M. Buckley, John A. Tuccillo, and Kevin E. Villani (Lexington, Mass.: Ballinger Publishing Co., 1977);

and George G. Kaufman and Gerard Albaum, "Variable Rate Residential Mortgages: Implications for Borrowers," in *Alternative Mortgage Instruments Research Study* (Washington, D.C.: Federal Home Loan Bank Board, 1977).

16. Variable-rate mortgages have been introduced and used widely in foreign countries, with the interest rate rising and falling with some index of market rates. See Modigliani and Lessard, *New Mortgage Designs for Stable Housing*, for summaries of foreign experience. Generally, since mortgage rates have varied freely with the market, periods of inflation and rapidly rising interest rates have brought these instruments into popular disfavor. This is especially true in England and Israel.

17. Clearly, if interest rates fell, borrowers could refinance. However, prepayment penalties are such that the lender could anticipate keeping a fixed rate loan for two or three years. VRM rates would be adjusted downward more quickly than that.

18. E. McFarlin and Thomas Vitek, "The Graduated Payment Mortgage," *Federal Home Loan Bank Board Journal*, vol. 13, no. 1 (January 1980) pp. 14–17, present specific evidence on the impact of GPMs in California. It should be noted that lender cooperation in the program has been induced by the creation of a secondary marketing facility for GPMs. Since 1978, graduated-payment mortgages have been included in GNMA pools. To the extent that the GPM originator is assured of a buyer for the mortgage, there is little objection to using it. Recently, however, pricing problems have reduced the effectiveness of this marketing facility.

19. For a complete analysis of the impact of mortgage revenue bonds on tax exempt, mortgage, and housing markets, and on productivity, see John A. Tuccillo and John C. Weicher, *Local Mortgage Revenue Bonds: Economic and Financial Issues* (Washington, D.C.: The Urban Institute, 1979); C. Duncan MacRae, David I. Rosenbaum, and John A. Tuccillo, "Mortgage Revenue Bonds and Metropolitan Housing Markets," Working Paper 1371-02 (Washington, D.C.: The Urban Institute, 1980); and Patric H. Hendershott, "Mortgage Revenue Bonds: Tax Avoidance with A Vengeance," Working Paper 1371-01 (Washington, D.C.: The Urban Institute, 1980).

NOTES TO CHAPTER 4

1. One can differentiate between the old system of ultimate investors being lenders ("institutional intermediation") and the more recent situation in which mortgages are repackaged as bonds or near-bonds ("security intermediation"). See Ernest Block, "Moving Mortgage Financing into the Capital Market: GNMA and Other Mortgage-Backed Issues" (New York: Salomon Brothers Center for the Study of Financial Institutions, New York University, 1980).

2. In fact, as stated in chapter 2, the federal government offered charters to private "national mortgage associations" in 1934. When no firm had stepped forward by 1938, the government entered the business itself.

3. While FNMA is not a federal agency, it enjoys a guaranteed line of credit to the Treasury. This line of credit causes FNMA debt to be considered as of federal quality and significantly reduces FNMA borrowing costs. In addition, FNMA is exempt from SEC-regulation requirements and their accompanying administrative costs.

4. See George G. Kaufman, "A Proposal for Eliminating Interest Rate Ceilings on Thrift Institutions," *Journal of Money, Credit, and Banking*, vol. 4, no. 3 (August 1972) pp. 735–43. FNMA can be thought of as an extremely large savings and loan and is therefore subject to many of the same stresses as these institutions.

5. Of course, FNMA never knew at the time of the auction the volume of mortgages that would be delivered. A forecast of future movements in mortgage rates was therefore necessary in order for FNMA to choose the level of commitments it issued (and therefore the size of its portfolio).

6. Leo Grebler, "The Role of the Public Sector in Residential Financing," in *Capital Markets and the Housing Sector*, ed. R.M. Buckley, John A. Tuccillo, and Kevin E. Villani (Lexington, Mass.: Ballinger Publishing Co., 1977). Extrapolation of their results, however, is dangerous, given the financial reforms that have occurred.

7. FHLMC in addition offered a bond-like instrument, the guaranteed mortgage certificate (GMC), which carried a fixed stream of payments, although collateralized by mortgages.

8. The reason most of these securities were held by financial intermediaries is owing, at least in part, to the regulation that allows savings and loans to count these holdings as qualified assets for tax and insurance purposes. A similar situation applies in the relationship of GNMAs to private pension funds.

9. The proper pricing of mortgage-backed securities, however, is a current issue in mortgage market analysis. See W. L. Silber, D.G. Black, and K.D. Garbade, "The Impact of the GNMA Pass-Through Program on FHA Mortgage Costs," Working Paper 216 (New York: Salomon Brothers Center for the Study of Financial Institutions, New York University, 1980).

Notes to Chapter 5

1. For a complete description, see Raymond J. Struyk, Neil Mayer, and John A. Tuccillo, chap. 8 in *Federal Housing Policy at Reagan's Mid-Term* (Washington, D.C.: The Urban Institute Press, 1983).

2. See John A. Tuccillo, "Structural Change and Federally Related Secondary Market Agencies," in *Structural Change in the Secondary Market* (Washington, D.C.: Federal National Mortgage Association, 1983).

3. Estimates by Office of Management and Budget, *Budget of the United States Government, Fiscal Year 1984, Special Analysis F* (Washington, D.C.: GPO), table F-1. The benefits of this federal connection have been estimated at various levels, most recently at 50 basis points by the President's Private Sector Survey on Cost Control.

4. This change reflects a considerable evolution. The suggestion first surfaced in the housing recession of 1974–1975 as an attempt to rationalize the FHA system. By the FY 1983 budget, it had become government policy.

5. The alternative types of mortgages allow lower mortgage payments, while the movement to a market-rate system removed the lump-sum payments (points) that are attached to FHA mortgages when administered rates lag market rates.

6. *Report of the President's Commission on Housing* (Washington, D.C.: GPO, 1982).

7. For a full description, see Andrew S. Carron, *The Plight of the Thrift Institutions* (Washington, D.C.: The Brookings Instituton, 1982); and Andrew S. Carron, *The Rescue of the Thrift Industry* (Washington, D.C.: The Brookings Institution, 1983).

8. For an analysis, see John A. Tuccillo, "The Economics of the Mortgage Tax Credit," *AREUEA Journal* (Summer 1983), forthcoming.

9. See Mark Meader, Larry Ozanne, and Donald Edwards, "Estimating the Impact of Due-On-Sale Restrictions on Savings and Loan Earnings" (Washington, D.C.: Federal Home Loan Bank Board, Office of Policy and Economic Research, 1982).

10. Testimony of David O. Maxwell before the Senate Subcommittee on Housing and Urban Affairs, U.S. Senate, May 5, 1983.

11. *OMB, Budget, Fiscal Year 1984*, pp. 5-55.

12. *Report of President's Commission on Housing*, chap. 12.

13. Ibid., p. 168.

14. Ibid., p. 167.

NOTES TO CHAPTER 6

1. It should be noted that the increasingly wide fluctuation in short-term rates may, in part, be traced to Federal Reserve policy actions. The October 1979 and March 1980 credit restrictions were correlated with increases in the amplitude of short-term rates.

2. David Seiders, "Major Developments in Residential Mortgage and Housing Markets since the Hunt Commission," *AREUEA Journal,* vol. 8, no. 1 (spring 1980), pp. 4–32, argues that the evolution of the housing finance system over the past decade is the result of the work of the Hunt Commission. Clearly, changes in the system that reflect the commission's recommendations have taken place, but direct causality is hard to assign. A variety of forces generated these changes.

3. For a concise summary of the legislative outgrowth of the Hunt Commission, see Kent W. Colton, "Financial Reform: A Review of the Past and Prospects for the Future," *AREUEA Journal*, vol. 8, no. 1 (spring 1980): pp. 91–117.

4. Note that with the abatement of inflation, the variable-rate mortgage becomes quite similar in cash flow to the standard mortgage. Thus, the ARM may be the dominant instrument, since it resembles the standard mortgage with no inflation but affords lenders a hedge against the occurrence of unanticipated inflation. The standard instrument, however, has staged a resurgence as inflation has fallen in the 1982–1983 period.

5. Projections reported in Richard G. Marcis and Dale Riordan, "The Savings and Loan Industry in the Eighties," *Federal Home Loan Bank Board Journal*, vol. 13, no. 8 (May 1980), pp. 2–15.

6. See Jay Janis, "The Winds of Change," *Federal Home Loan Bank Board Journal* (August 1980), pp. 2–3; and Dennis J. Jacobe and Brian Smith, "The Impact of New Liability Instruments on Thrifts and Housing," paper presented at the annual meeting of the Allied Social Sciences Association, Chicago, 1978.

7. James E. McNulty and William E. Chalker, "The Forward Commitment Market for Mortgage Backed Securities," *Federal Home Loan Bank Board Journal*, vol. 13, no. 6 (June 1980), pp. 2–15, in an analysis of savings and loans' misuse of the mortgage commitment process to generate income, provide an interesting commentary on the reeducation needed by these institutions. Essentially, a number of associations have attempted to cover declining profitability by selling commitments to buy mortgages as much as two years in the future. Commitment income offsets current expenses; however, when commitments come due, the association may have to buy mortgages at prices far above the current market.

8. That education is proceeding slowly. See Kenneth D. Noble, "Thrift Units: Cautious Rivals," *New York Times*, May 23, 1983, pp. D1, D4.

9. Testimony of David O. Maxwell before the House Subcommittee on Housing and Community Development, U.S. House of Representatives, June 3, 1982.

10. *Report of the President's Commission on Housing* (Washington, D.C.: GPO, 1982), pp. 166–167.

11. One prominent study, Patric Hendershott and Keven E. Villani, *Regulation and Reform of the Housing Finance System* (Washington, D.C.: American Enterprise Institute, 1977), concluded that over the period 1965 to 1971, interest rates were reduced by about one percentage point. On the other hand, five-sixths of the mortgage purchases by the federal agencies were offset by reduced purchases from private institutions, so that the net effect on the amount of mortgage credit was slight.

12. Leo Grebler, "An Assessment of the Performance of the Public Sector in the Residential Housing Market: 1955–1974," in *Capital Markets and the Housing Sector*, ed. R. Buckley, John A. Tucillo, and Kevin E. Villani (Lexington, Mass: Ballinger Books, 1977), pp. 311–346.

13. Somewhat perversely, there may at the same time be an increase in the amount of credit supplied through the secondary market. That is, if FNMA and FHLMC have been offering fewer securities than the market clearing level at that price, then even with a constant demand and upward shifting supply curve for mortgage funds from the secondary market, the level of secondary market financing actually provided may increase.

14. U.S. Department of Housing and Urban Development, "A Study of a GNMA Conventional Mortgage Pass-Through Security Program," by R. Van Order and Kevin E. Villani, in *Occasional Papers in Housing and Community Affairs*, vol. 9 (Washington, D.C.: GPO, March 1981), pp. 155–192.

15. This adjustment process will not fall into place immediately. Those institutions used to living under regulation will need time to develop the mechanisms to compete in general financial markets. To give an example, in both 1966 and 1969, savings and loans would have been financially incapable of competing for funds with other borrowers when interest rates shot up, because of the sufficient mortgage revenues of these institutions and their low levels of net worth.

16. Increased merger activity has implications for the insurance system covering financial intermediaries. Under current practice, solvency problems are tolerated by the market because of the implicit net-worth subsidy afforded by deposit insurance. If weaker associations are merged into larger associations, the insurance subsidy to remaining institutions will fall and the premium structure—and perhaps the entire system—will need to be revised. For a discussion of this, see Edward J. Kane, "Savings and Loan Diversification and Housing Finance Under Deregulation," in *Savings and Loan Asset Management Under Deregulation* (San Francisco: Federal Home Loan Bank of San Francisco, 1981).